Texas Indian Myths and Legends

Jane Archer

Texas Indian Myths and Legends

Jane Archer

Republic of Texas Press

Published by Republic of Texas Press
An imprint of The Rowman & Littlefield Publishing Group, Inc.
4501 Forbes Boulevard, Suite 200
Lanham, MD 20706 ,

Distributed by NATIONAL BOOK NETWORK

Library of Congress Cataloging-in-Publication Data

Archer, Jane.
    Texas Indian myths and legends / Jane Archer.
      p. cm.
    Includes bibliographical references.
    ISBN 1-55622-725-6 (pbk.)
    1. Indians of North America—Texas—Folklore. 2. Indian mythology—Texas.
3. Legends—Texas. I. Title.

F78.T4 A73   2000   99-051935
398.2'089'970764—dc21   CIP

For Tall Trees,
who asked that I remember.

Acknowledgement

At Republic of Texas Press, Dianne Stultz, Production Editor, and Ginnie Siena Bivona, Acquisition Editor, gave freely of their time, expertise, and support to help make this the best book possible.

C. Dean Andersson, novelist and technical writer, kept the home fires burning and food in the refrigerator. He read every page, bless his heart, as it came out of the computer, then gave expert editorial advice.

DeWitt King Jr. and Stella McIntosh Dennis inspired me to keep digging for more myths and more history, so that in the next volume I can include their very own Choctaw.

Special thanks go to the wonderful staff of the Richardson Public Library in Richardson, Texas. Marilyn Comte, Interlibrary Loan Staff, and Linda Lee and Mike Furl, Information Desk Librarians, truly worked miracles in locating sources for this book. They kept my book bag full of goodies, and that is my highest praise for a library.

Table of Contents

Contents

List of Illustrations

Texas Indian Pictographs

This design used throughout the book is based on the Indian pictographs located on the face of a cliff near Onion Creek in Doss Valley of Gillespie County, once deep in the Comanche southern hunting ground. These messages were painted in red, green, and white from six to twenty-five inches in height to tell many stories.

Introduction

Imagine ancient myths and legends set to song, drum, and dance. Imagine flickering campfires and the scent of wood smoke on a summer breeze. Imagine twinkling stars and moonlight in a vast dark sky. Imagine the sacred story of your people, your religion, your heritage told by your elders in a language that rings truthfully in your ears.

Now imagine many years ago but not so far away in the land of the Caddo, the Lipan Apache, the Wichita, the Comanche, the Alabama-Coushatta. Texas.

If you can imagine it, then it exists. Now as then. From catching a dance at the Alabama-Coushatta Indian Reservation near Livingston, Texas, to snatching a quick Comanche buffalo burger in Fort Sill, Oklahoma, myths and legends are still told around campfires. I retell many of them right here in this book, and I also include a brief history of each tribe.

I grew up collecting flint arrowheads on Arrowhead Hill deep in the Piney Woods of East Texas, but I also collected stories like the one about Blue Hole. My friends and I were told to stay away from Blue Hole, a former camp of the Caddo, because it was bottomless and a child who swam there might never return. Naturally that made Blue Hole all the better, and many years later I used Blue Hole as the pivotal point in a novel.

As a storyteller, I owe a debt of gratitude to collectors John R. Swanton, George A. Dorsey, Morris Edward Opler, Howard N. Martin, Herwanna Becker Barnard, and the tribal elders who shared myths and legends with them.

Their stories open a window into a world of humor, religion, pathos, valor, love, and honor.

The myths and legends in this book were collected between the years 1900 and 1940 on the Alabama-Coushatta Reservation in Texas, on the Mescalero Apache Reservation in New Mexico, in Louisiana, and in post-reservation Oklahoma. Many of the stories were later published in journals and books.

I read through these publications, selected myths and legends that I believed best depicted the people who created them, then rewrote the stories in a more contemporary style. I used only myths and legends that have previously appeared in print because many tribal stories are sacred and secret.

No doubt the myths were altered by storytellers over time in response to a changing world. Tonin, a Caddo male deity, most likely was once Tonatsin, Our Mother. Yet the spirit of the legends remains the same and reveals the distinctions between the tribes. In "Deer Medicine," the Comanche sense of humor takes center stage in the story of a walk-up fast-food deer cave. I still laugh when I think of this myth, and I've been known to pick up a stick and say, "One fat buffalo."

Millions of indigenous people lived in the Lone Star State before the European and Anglo-American invasions, and they developed diverse cultures over many generations that continue to speak through their myths and legends.

In the following map I indicate general areas for the tribes I include in this book. They all had definite boundaries, but those changed as Eastern Indians resettled west and the Anglo-American invasion intensified. Comanche bands claimed territory from south Texas to the Canadian River in Oklahoma. Wichitas built villages from Waco north to the Red River. Lipan Apaches lived for a time on the Gulf Coast, but they also roamed far west and south into Mexico. And Caddos ruled East Texas until they shared their territory with immigrant Alabama-Coushattas.

As I researched this book, as well as my own part-Comanche heritage, I found so much material that a second volume is already in the works to include other native nations of Texas.

Comanches

Wichitas

Caddos

Alabama-Coushattas

Lipan Apaches

Indians of Texas 1830

Caddo Confederacies

This design is based on a common motif in Southeastern Indian water-serpent transport myths featuring Horned Water Snake.

Myths and Legends

The Origin of Animals

In the beginning of the world, people and animals lived together in trust and respect. There was no difference between them. Yet after a time their numbers increased until not enough food grew for them all.

They called a council and decided that some should become animals and be hunted as food by those who remained people.

The ones who lived where wildfire burned off prairie grass and who agreed to become animals rolled in the dark ashes until they turned black. They rolled a final time and became bears. They used long shards of white rock for claws and teeth.

The bears received ten lives. After dying the first time, they rose from the ground where their blood spilled for another life. Gentle in the first life, they became more fierce with each death until by the tenth life they fought and ate people.

Others who lived in the tall grass rolled upon the ground and rose up in the form of buffalo. The grass stuck to them and hung under their heads as beards. They also received ten lives to live on the plains where they would be hunted by people.

Deer formed the same way and then one animal after another until all the beasts roamed across the Earth.

The Prediction of Tonin

After the people came to the surface of the Earth, Tonin joined them. Only four feet tall, Tonin rode a bay horse the size of a dog. He could turn dark to light. If he wished to travel a long distance, he would be there at once. If he wished to kill game, he need only point a finger and the animal fell dead. He could grant every wish, and he could predict the future.

Yet frequently he vanished, and the people sought him in vain. Once they saw him rise high into the vast blue sky.

One day Tonin sent a crier out to the people. He called them to council because he had a great announcement. When the people assembled around him, he talked for half a day. He told them about their world and then explained that he would leave and be gone for six winters and six summers. He wanted them to meet him again in six days to watch him begin his journey.

In six days, the people grouped around him. He sang the song of death, then gradually rose upward into the sky. The people cried when they could no longer see him, for they feared he would never return. Yet they took courage from his promise to come back to them.

After three summers and three winters, the people began to forget Tonin and his words. As time passed the world changed, and even the stars grew bigger and brighter.

One of Tonin's six brothers knew it was time for Tonin's return, so he beat six times on his drum to remind the people. Yet not everyone remembered the meaning of the signal.

That evening a bright star rose in the east, and the

people gathered to watch it. Tonin descended, pleased to see the people waiting for him. He talked to them half the night, telling them about the future.

Tonin warned them that a strange race of people would come into the land and frighten away the buffalo, the deer, and the bear.

He stayed on Earth awhile, then assembled the people again. He explained that he would leave as he had before, but he would never return.

Blessing the people, he rose into the sky.

Evening Star and Orphan Star

Orphan wanted to hunt and play with the other boys, but he was poor and alone. He lived with a large family who tolerated him only so long as he did all the hard work. Every time the people moved camp his family tried to leave him behind, but he always found them because he had no other place to go.

One day Orphan rode with several families on boats to an island in a large lake. He hoped this special invitation to hunt eggs meant they were finally accepting him. He had a good time playing and gathering eggs. Later he listened with the others to stories as they ate eggs around a campfire.

In the morning Orphan awoke to find the others gone. He searched the island for them, but he knew they had filled their boats with eggs and left him behind to starve.

He was more alone than ever before in his young life, but he was determined to survive. He realized he had no bow and arrows to hunt. He tried to catch fish with his hands, but they swam away. As days passed, he ate scraps from the campfires, found a few eggs, and sat by the water's edge. He looked toward the mainland in despair, because it was too far away for him to swim and no boats made their way toward him.

After a time he noticed ripples in the water, then Horned Water Snake, known as Horned Monster, broke the surface in a loud splash. The creature glided close. Orphan sat still, too frightened to move.

"I am here to save you," Horned Monster said.

Orphan stared at the huge creature, too frightened to speak.

"I saw those people leave you here, but I take pity on you. Get on my back, hold onto my horns, and I will carry you safely to the mainland."

Orphan could hardly contain his joy. Someone finally cared enough to save him. He no longer felt fear. He climbed onto Horned Monster's back, clutching two of the three horns.

"One request," Horned Monster said. "Keep watch on the blue sky. If you see a star, quickly tell me."

"I will watch," Orphan said.

They started out across the lake, but they had not gone far when Orphan saw a star.

"Up there! I see a star in the west." Orphan pointed upward.

Horned Monster raised a mighty head, looked up, then turned around and swam swiftly back to shore.

"We will try again tomorrow," Horned Monster said.

Orphan reluctantly stepped back onto the island and

watched the creature disappear under the water.

Bright and early the next morning, Orphan returned to the shore to await Horned Monster. Soon he rode on the mighty creature toward the mainland. They were only a little farther than the day before when he saw a star again.

"There!" He pointed toward the sky. "I see a star in the west."

Horned Monster turned around and swam back to the island. Orphan jumped off and watched the creature disappear beneath the water.

Discouraged but still hopeful, Orphan found a few seeds and nuts and an egg to eat, then he sat down to wait.

The next day they started out again and got father than they had the day before. Orphan watched the sky, hoping not to see a star. Soon he saw the star again. He thought about not telling Horned Monster, but the creature was his only way to leave the island and he did not want to take a chance on losing his ride so far from either shore.

He slowly raised his arm and pointed. "Up there. I see a star in the west."

Horned Monster turned around and swam faster than ever back to the island. Orphan hopped off and watched the creature disappear beneath the surface of the water.

Orphan scrounged a few more bites of food, then sat down to wait, lonely and hungry.

Horned Monster arrived the next day and again the next four days. Each day they swam closer to the mainland shore, but each day they returned to the island at the first sight of the star. Orphan slowly starved, hope fading a little more with each return to the island.

On the sixth day they were within a few feet of the mainland shore when Orphan saw the star. He was so anxious to reach land that for the first time he said nothing, because he knew the creature would take him straight back to the island.

As Horned Monster swam almost into shallow water, Orphan watched the star. He saw a huge black cloud roll in front of the star. Frightened, he jumped off, but just as he did something struck the creature and Horned Monster rolled over dead.

Orphan swam to shore and saw a handsome young man standing there.

"You did me a great favor," the man said. "Horned Monster made the lake dangerous for people, so for a long time I tried to kill the creature."

"Horned Monster saved me."

"You lured Horned Monster out so I had a chance I never had before. Thank you."

Orphan looked down at his only friend, now dead because of him. "I want Horned Monster's sacrifice to live on in people's stories."

"The creature will not be forgotten." The young man looked up at the sky. "For your help, I will take you to the sky with me. Would you like to go?"

Orphan looked at Horned Monster then at his new friend. "Yes. I have no one else here."

The young man clasped Orphan's hand, then they sailed into the sky.

After that day the people looked up into the bright blue sky to see Orphan Star standing without fail beside Evening Star.

Maiden's Wish Upon a Star

Once long ago, Maiden, a beautiful young woman, wanted something more in her life. She longed to travel, for she was lonely even with her family and her people. Her older sisters were married, but she found no one who suited her.

One summer night she lay in an arbor and watched the stars in the sky. They were beautiful and far away. She noticed they were not all alike. Some twinkled brightly while others remained dim. As she watched, one appealed to her more than the others. North Star was the brightest and most beautiful of all.

"Spirits, help me," she prayed. "I wish to go somewhere else. I wish to wed North Star and live as his wife in the night sky above."

She felt the light of North Star bathe her in beauty and wonder.

"Spirits, I pray to you. Let me marry North Star. It is the only way I will ever be happy."

She closed her eyes to dream of the wonderful event in her sleep.

When she awoke she looked around and blinked in confusion. She lay beside a campfire. An ancient man sat nearby, watching her.

"Where am I?" she asked. "Who are you?"

"Your wish is granted," he said. "I am North Star, your husband."

"But North Star is beautiful, the most beautiful of all in the sky."

"As are you. Do we not suit each other well?"

Tears filled her eyes, for this North Star did not fit her

dream at all. He could only be the great-grandfather of her strong young hunter, a man who would give her many beautiful children.

In the days that followed, North Star remained a wise elder who happily shared his home with her. She realized she had little interest in the stars, North Star in particular, and she longed to get away. But her wish had been granted, so she quietly tended a garden, cooked, and made baskets.

While she worked, she plotted to escape. She tried several different routes, but they all led back to North Star. Frustrated, she thought and thought.

"Are you happy here?" North Star asked one day.

"I have everything I need."

"Good. When you work in the garden be careful not to move that big round stone."

"Why not?"

"It is dangerous. I do not want you hurt."

"I will be careful."

For several days she avoided the stone. Yet the more she walked around it, the more she wanted to touch it. Finally she let a fingertip trail across its smooth surface. Nothing happened. Emboldened, she laid her palm against it. Nothing happened. She rubbed hard with her hand. Still nothing happened. Pleased with her success, she went on about her work.

One day when North Star left to visit neighbors, she hurried to the garden and stood before the stone. She could no longer resist the temptation. She rolled the stone away. A hole yawned underneath. She gazed into it and saw all the way to Earth. She longed to return to her real home, but she was too far away to ever get there. She rolled the stone back in place.

When North Star returned, he looked at her. "You did not move that stone, did you?"

"I worked safely in the garden."

"Good. Remember that stone is dangerous."

As she cooked that night, she thought and thought. She realized she had made a mistake by wishing to marry North Star, but the only way to correct it was through the hole under the rock in the garden. She had to get back to Earth. She thought some more. If she could make a rope long enough, perhaps she could climb down it to home. She knew her people had once made ropes out of soapweeds, so maybe she could too.

When North Star left for his nightly trip through the sky, she hurried outside and found a stand of soapweeds. She cut soapweeds all night long and then hurried home before he returned. Each night he traveled through the sky and she cut soapweeds. They ate together when he returned, so he never suspected her new wish.

When she finally gathered enough soapweeds, she began making the rope. She worked hard, night after night, but she never told her husband because she feared he might not want her to go.

When she believed she had a rope long enough to reach Earth, she carried it to the garden. She rolled the stone away, then let the rope down, playing it out until she finally came to the end. She tied it to the rock and placed the rock back over the hole.

She arrived home just in time to greet North Star after his journey through the sky. They ate together. She wished he could be the man of her dreams, but now she wanted only to return to Earth.

When North Star sailed across the sky the next evening, she left a special basket made of soapweeds for him, then hurried to the garden. She rolled the stone away and started climbing down the rope. She continued down a long time before she finally saw land. Yet she grew tired and feared she might never reach Earth. Abruptly the rope ended. She hung near treetops, but she could not get down and she was too weak to go up. She clung there between sky and Earth as she thought about what to do.

A bird cry roused her from her thoughts. She saw a large bird swoop overhead, then under her. On the fourth pass, the bird spoke to her.

"If you step onto my back," he said, "I will carry you home."

"Thank you. I come from far away and my arms will not hold me much longer."

The bird flew under her and she stepped down onto a softly feathered back.

"Are you ready?" he asked.

"Yes."

"Let go of the rope. I will not drop you."

She hesitated for only a moment before deciding to trust. She dropped the rope and grabbed for feathers.

Wide wings caught air currents as the bird gently flew downward toward land.

"May I take you home?" he asked.

"Oh yes. I wish to be no place else, except perhaps on your great back."

With several flaps of wide wings, he lowered her to the ground near her village. She stepped down, then she gently touched his sharp beak with her fingertips.

"You are safe now," he said. "I must return to my own home as you must to yours."

"Thank you."

He spread massive wings and lifted into the sky.

Remember.

"Remember. I am Black Eagle."

As she watched him fly away, she prayed he would soon return.

Orphan Boy Gets Power

Orphan Boy lived with his grandfather after his parents died when he was a baby, and they spent many happy years together. When Orphan Boy neared the age when Grandfather would make him a bow and arrows and teach him to hunt, Grandfather died. Orphan Boy mourned the loss of his only friend and family.

With no way to hunt for food, Orphan Boy begged at one lodge then another. He gave thanks for the generosity of the people, but at night he returned alone to his lodge. He cried himself to sleep, fearful of his loneliness and poverty.

He did not grow as strong as the other boys in the village, and he did not know how to play with them when they came to visit. They teased him and laughed at him because he was sad and lonely, and they always threw him when they wrestled.

Yet Orphan Boy grew brave and courageous. In a few years, he made a bow and arrows. He practiced, then went out to hunt. He learned quickly and brought back small game. He felt happy because he no longer had to beg food from others.

One day when he hunted alone in the woods, he heard a voice calling him. Puzzled, he stopped and listened. A boy about his age ran out of the brush. The stranger ran around with so much fun and energy that Orphan Boy wanted him for a friend.

They played together for a time, then they decided to see who was the stronger. The stranger appeared more powerful, but Orphan Boy soon learned that he could throw his new friend.

"I do not understand," Orphan Boy said. "All the boys in the village make fun of me because they are stronger and can throw me. Yet I can throw you."

The stranger rose from the ground. "I watched the other boys tease and throw you, but you never lost courage. I am powerful, and I gave that strength to you."

Orphan Boy lifted a huge rock, amazed at his sudden power.

"You are now one of the strongest men in the world," the stranger said. "You may go back to your village and throw any of the other boys."

As night descended, the stranger stepped into the brush and disappeared.

Orphan Boy decided to sleep in the forest since he could not find his way home in the dark. At dawn he arose with renewed strength and hunted. He killed three deer and then headed back to his village. Even with his new power, the load was heavy and he moved slowly. The sun set again before he reached home, so he lay down to rest.

"Will you go to the meeting place where the other boys wrestle?" The stranger stepped out of the woods.

"I must carry this load home so I have no time."

"Let me help you."

They carried the three deer together, and soon they reached the meeting place. Many boys and men were there.

"Wrestle me." A boy stepped forward.

Orphan Boy set down his deer and wrestled the boy. He quickly threw him, then again and again.

The boys and men grew afraid, so they left Orphan Boy alone with his friend.

They sat down together, and the stranger told Orphan Boy more about his power and how to use it. At dawn, the stranger disappeared again.

Orphan Boy picked up his three deer and walked home. After a few days he heard that the other boys planned to compete in wrestling matches. He went to watch, but he stayed back with the spectators.

One of the wrestlers saw him. "Wrestle with us if you are not afraid."

Orphan Boy shook his head.

"Coward!" the young man taunted. "You are weak. You do not want to lose."

Orphan Boy threw off his blanket and ran into the ring. He threw the young man hard and he died.

"I will wrestle any of you," Orphan Boy cried.

He tried to get others to fight him, but nobody else would because now they all feared him.

As word of his strength spread, Orphan Boy gained the respect of all the people.

She-Who-Calls-the-Buffalo

She-Who-Calls-the-Buffalo lived with her six brothers in a lodge in the woods. At night her brothers left to travel through the sky, for they were bright stars. They returned each morning, told her of their adventures, then put her in a swing made of lariat rope that hung from the sky.

They swung her through the air, higher and higher. When the buffalo saw her swing, they came running to her. Sending arrows swiftly through the air, her brothers killed all the buffalo they wanted, then the rest of the herd went away. This way the family never went hungry.

One day Coyote stopped by for a visit, and he noticed that meat and corn were always plenty.

"I would like to live with you," Coyote said.

"Yes do," She-Who-Calls-the-Buffalo said. "My brothers are gone a lot and I get lonely."

Suspicious, the brothers decided to let Coyote stay with them. Coyote told fine stories to She-Who-Calls-the-Buffalo in the evenings when her star brothers rode through the sky. They ate plenty of buffalo meat, but after a time Coyote grew curious.

"You get plenty of meat," Coyote said. "How do you do it?"

The brothers held council and decided to show Coyote the trick of the swing.

"We will let you watch the buffalo come, but first you must promise never to do what we do while we are gone."

"I agree," Coyote said.

Early the next morning the brothers allowed Coyote to watch them swing their sister. The buffalo came as usual.

"That is impressive," Coyote said. "I want to do it too."

"No," the eldest brother said. "If others swing her, they will swing her too hard and she will never return."

"I can swing as good as you," Coyote said.

"You must promise never to swing her," another brother said.

"I agree," Coyote said.

One day the brothers were gone and Coyote sought out She-Who-Calls-the-Buffalo.

"I want to swing you," Coyote said.

"No. It is not safe," she said.

"I will swing you, or I will hurt your brothers and you."

She knew Coyote to be strong and powerful. "If you insist, you may swing me, but be careful not to swing me to high or too hard."

"I agree," Coyote said.

She sat down in the swing and Coyote pushed her. The buffalo did not come. Coyote pushed harder. She swung higher. The buffalo still did not come. Coyote pushed even harder. She swung higher and higher until she disappeared.

"Come back," Coyote called, suddenly afraid. "If you do not come back, I will jump up and get you."

She did not reappear. The buffalo did not come. Coyote grumbled and growled.

Later the star brothers came home and looked for their sister. She was nowhere to be found.

"Coyote," the eldest said. "Where is She-Who-Calls-the-Buffalo?"

"I do not know, but I believe some monster, perhaps a cannibal, carried her away."

The brothers knew at once that Coyote lied.

"You put her in the swing and swung her too high," the eldest said.

"Not me," Coyote said.

"You go away," another brother said.

"You lied and tricked us," the eldest brother said. "You and your children will now go hungry."

As Coyote trudged away, the six brothers turned to each other for council.

"I miss my sister," one brother said.

"So do I," another agreed.

"Let us join her in the sky," the eldest said.

So the star brothers went to the sky and live there today with She-Who-Calls-the-Buffalo.

Mother-of-All-the-Pecan-Trees

An elder woman owned all the pecan trees, so she harvested the nuts and kept them to herself. The people had to go to her lodge to get the delicious pecans. She would give them a few to eat, but she would never let them take any back home.

After a time the people grew hungry. They knew Mother-of-All-the-Pecan-Trees had a lodge full of pecans. They wanted her to share more nuts with them. Yet she still only gave them a few, insisting they eat them before they left her lodge. Finally the people became angry, and they decided to take the pecans away from her.

In the village of Field Rats, four young boys plagued

their father and everyone else with their wild ways. The people decided these boys were the ones to steal nuts from Mother-of-All-the-Pecan-Trees. They reasoned that the boys were small and sly, and the people would only be rid of a nuisance if the elder woman killed them. The boys agreed to go because they always liked trouble.

One boy set off to spy on Mother-of-All-the-Pecan-Trees. He peeked through a small opening in her lodge. She still worked, so he waited until she went to bed that night. When he heard snores, he knew it was time to steal pecans. He hurried back to his father's lodge.

"She sleeps." The boy raced inside and then stopped in surprise.

Coyote sat there.

"Don't bother to steal pecans," Coyote said. "I will kill Mother-of-All-the-Pecan-Trees tomorrow."

The rat brothers clicked their sharp teeth together in disappointment. They wanted to steal pecans.

"Soon we will all have plenty of nuts." Coyote wanted to get there first and take the most pecans.

Early the next morning Coyote trotted over to the lodge of Mother-of-All-the-Pecan-Trees.

She sorted pecans in front of her lodge.

"Good morning," Coyote said. "What a beautiful day."

"Yes it is." She stopped work to watch Coyote.

"I am very hungry. I crave a few of your pecans."

She gave Coyote a few nuts.

Coyote quickly ate them. "Delicious. May I have a few more? Perhaps some from inside your lodge."

She turned to get them. Coyote pulled out a stone knife and hit her on the head. She fell over, spilling pecans across the ground.

After she died, pecan trees grew everywhere and belonged to all the people.

Path-of-the-Cyclone

Early one morning a young man took his daily bath, then he sat on the riverbank to watch the sun rise in the east. He listened to the songs of birds, the wind in the trees, and the plop of frogs into the water. The scent of pine swirled around him as a voice spoke in his ear.

"I know your grandmother sends you here to bathe every morning, no matter how hot or cold, so that you will grow strong with endurance. You proved yourself to me. Now I am willing to give you more strength, more power than is even in your dreams."

Surprised, the young man looked about for the source of the voice, but he saw nothing beyond the usual tranquil scene. He shrugged, then went back to admiring sunlight glittering over the surface of the river.

A man slowly rose from the water. "I am Power-of-the-Cyclone."

The young man felt no fright, only curiosity.

"Face the west as you always do and dive into the river four times," Power-of-the-Cyclone said.

The young man followed the instructions exactly, then sat back down on the bank.

"Once I was powerful enough to hold the mighty winds in my control," Power-of-the-Cyclone said. "People feared me. Now I grow older and my strength wanes."

The young man felt the wind stir weakly around him.

"I looked the world over for someone to take my place, someone who could properly handle my powers. I almost gave up before I found you."

The young man grew excited. He leaned forward to learn more.

"I will give my power to you. Stand up."

The young man stood up.

"Swing your arms around."

The young man swung his arms, faster and faster.

Soon a huge black cloud rolled down from the north, then turned to pass west. The young man swung his arms harder and faster. Wind broke away from the cloud and cut a wide swath through the forest, ripping up trees by their roots and sending the river into a boiling fury.

"Stop," Power-of-the-Cyclone yelled. "Don't move your arms."

The young man lowered his arms and looked around in astonishment while he panted as if running hard.

"You now have my power, but never abuse it."

The young man inclined his head in respect.

"You need only send the cyclone in the spring when it is necessary. I grant you a new name. Path-of-the-Cyclone. All the people will know you by this name."

Power-of-the-Cyclone disappeared back under the water, and the river became calm once more.

After that the people recognized the young man's power when they saw him sail through the sky on the crest of a cyclone.

ᐃᶓ•ʹ∼∼∼ᶓᐅ

Ten Brothers and the Cannibals

Grandmother kept a safe and warm home for her ten grandsons. She told them stories around the fire at night, and they played during the day. They also farmed and hunted, providing plenty of food for the family.

One day the oldest brother went out to hunt, but he did not return. Grandmother worried about him, so the next day another brother went in search of him. He did not return either. Grandmother worried even more, so another brother went to find the first two boys. And so it went until the ninth brother failed to return.

Grandmother and the youngest boy waited and waited. With deep sadness in their hearts, they continued to work but they no longer played. They hoped to hear something about the other nine, but no word came to them. They grew sadder every day.

"I can wait no longer," the youngest boy said. "I must find my lost brothers."

"Oh no," Grandmother said. "You are all I have left. What if you never return? I will die of heartbreak."

"But they may await rescue."

"I fear whatever evil happened to them will happen to you."

"I must take a chance."

"You are too young to go alone into the woods."

"They are too young to be lost. I will find them."

He hugged Grandmother close, then prepared to go. She packed food for him. He prayed for guidance. As he left home, he stuck an eagle feather in his hair, hoping it held hidden power to help him.

After walking a long time and far away, he saw a tepee in the distance. He crept near it and heard people talking inside.

"Another comes," a man said. "Cook some corn for we will soon have meat."

The boy understood what the man meant, but he was so sad, tired, and hungry that he no longer cared if he lived or died. He walked right up to the tepee.

A man wearing a facemask with a sharp iron nose came outside. "You look thin. Did you travel far?"

"Yes."

"Are you looking for your nine brothers?"

"Yes."

"I know where your brothers are now. I will even set you on the right trail to find them. First you must work for me. Will you do that?"

"Yes."

"See that big log over there?"

"Yes."

"Pick it up and put it on the fire."

The boy did not want to do anything the man suggested, but he thought maybe some power would help him.

"I will give you four trials. If you cannot lift the log, you must lay down on it and let me lift it."

The boy trusted nothing he heard, but he prayed for help to rescue his brothers. He tried to lift the log four times, straining and groaning and heaving, but he was not strong enough to move it.

"Now you must lay down and let me move it," the man said.

Reluctantly the boy kept his word.

As the man lowered his face to spear the boy with the iron nose of the mask, an unseen power jerked the boy off the log. The iron nose caught in the log and held the man so he could not get free.

"Boy, run into the tepee and take the corn pounder away from the woman in there," a voice on the wind said. "Kill her, then bring it here and beat this man to death." The boy jumped to his feet and followed the instructions exactly. When the man lay dead at his feet, he listened for the voice again.

"Go back inside the tepee. There you will find the bones of your bothers." A young man appeared beside the boy. "I will help you gather them."

Soon they carried the bones outside, and the young man sorted them into nine piles."

"Now put your buffalo robe over them," the young man said. "After that shoot an arrow up into the sky and cry, 'Look out, brothers, the arrow will hit you!'"

Again the boy followed the instructions exactly, and his brothers jumped out from under the robe.

"Now burn the tepee with the man and woman inside it, then scatter the ashes," the young man said.

The ten brothers quickly finished the task.

"I am the Sun. I helped you destroy the cannibals. Now return to your grandmother." The young man disappeared in a flash of golden light.

The brothers hurried home. Grandmother greeted them with tears of joy. That night beside the fire they told her their story. "The Sun took pity and helped me," the youngest boy finished.

Thereafter the people knew the Sun was their friend and would always help them in times of trouble.

ᎦᏣ•ᎳᎳᎳᏓᏣᎾ

Death of a Cannibal

One day at Tall-Timber-on-Top-of-the-Hill the people agreed to move to another village. As they packed, a woman whose husband had died gave birth to their child. She could not travel on such a long journey with her new baby. The people could not wait for her. They left her to follow when she regained her strength.

For many days she stayed alone with her baby in the village. She longed to be with her people. She shivered in fear at animal cries in the night. She grew more anxious to be gone with each setting of the sun.

One night she sat in her grass lodge rocking her baby in her arms. Flames from a warm fire cast menacing shadows on the walls. She listened for danger.

"Let me come inside," a man called from outside the lodge.

She shivered in fright. "Did my people send you?"

"No. You may trust me because I often stay near their village at night."

She felt so lonely that she overcame her fear. "Come inside."

A tall stranger entered the lodge and sat down across the fire from her. "I am Spotted Wolf. I feel concern for the safety of you and your child."

"Do not worry for us."

"You must not start your journey too soon. Many dangerous animals lurk in the woods."

"I hear them at night, but I must go to my people soon."

"Your life is in danger if you go now."

"I dare not wait much longer."

He handed her a leather pouch. "If trouble finds you, toss a pinch of this tobacco to the four directions, then call me. I will help you."

"Thank you." She watched him leave, clutching the tobacco pouch to her baby.

Several days later she placed her baby in a cradle board on her back, then started on her journey. At dusk on the third day, a strange being blocked her path. As she walked closer, she could not decide if it were man or beast.

The stranger fell to the ground, rolled over twice, and arose as an animal. She closed her eyes and shook her head to make sure she saw correctly. When she looked again, the animal was a person.

Now she knew great fear, for the creature must surely be a cannibal. They appeared as humans, then they turned into wild beasts and ate people. She could not move for her fear, sure that she and her baby would be eaten.

The cannibal growled and then stalked toward her.

She remembered Spotted-Wolf. She pulled out the pouch he gave her, then she tossed a pinch of tobacco to the south, the west, the north, and the east.

"Spotted Wolf, please help me and my baby." She repeated her request four times.

A wolf howled in the south, another in the west, one in the north, and finally in the east. She sighed in relief.

The cannibal looked around in fright, growls tapering to a whine.

A large spotted wolf came running toward them from each direction. The four wolves lunged forward together and killed the cannibal.

The wolf from the south escorted the woman and her

baby safely to her new village, then disappeared back into the woods.

Arrows for a Ghost

Two hunters left their village before dawn one morning and walked far in search of game. They hunted long and hard all day, but they caught nothing. When night darkened the land around them, they decided to sleep in the timber so they could get up and hunt the next day. They refused to return home empty-handed.

As they slept on beds of soft grass, they abruptly awoke to the sound of a whooping voice.

One hunter leaped to his feet in fear and raced for home through the darkness.

The other hunter had never run away in fear, so he bravely stood up.

A ghost drifted toward him.

"May I help you enter Spirit Land?" the brave hunter asked.

"I try and I try, but my bowstring has a knot in it and I can go no farther," the ghost said. "Will you give me a bowstring and make me two new arrows?"

"Yes, I will help you." The hunter sat down and started to make two arrows.

The ghost laid his bow beside the hunter and hovered anxiously nearby.

The hunter finished the arrows, then he put a new string on the bow. He handed them to the ghost.

"Thank you," the ghost said. "When I am in the air, I will whoop to let you know the arrows carried me high. You whoop back to let me know you heard."

The ghost shot the arrows into the sky, and they carried him upward.

Listening closely, the hunter heard a whoop from the ghost, so he whooped back. He waited, but he heard no more so he knew the ghost was safely in Spirit Land.

He returned to his village the next day and told his people about the ghost.

Since that time the people make and bury bows and arrows with the dead, so ghosts go straight to Spirit Land and do not wander the Earth. Yet they never make bows and arrows at night because the activity might attract a ghost and cause a death in the family.

Giant Turtle

One day after a great council, the people decided they needed a new village. They broke camp and started a long search for the best place. After a time they reached a large lake with a giant rock near the shore. They thought the rock would make a good dance area, so they built their village near it.

They held several powerful dances on the rock, and everyone was pleased with the site of their village. They continued to live happily as before.

Sometime later a crier ran to all the lodges and announced a big dance. The people assembled on the giant rock and danced to drum and rattle and flute. Soon they were surprised to feel the rock move. They stopped and looked down to see a big head and four legs appear from underneath it.

They realized their dance floor was not a rock but a giant turtle. They tried to get away, but their feet stuck to the turtle's shell. They screamed for help, pulled at their feet to get free, but they could not move.

The giant turtle dove deep into the water and carried the people to their death.

Rabbit Steals Mountain Lion's Teeth

One day after Grandmother left to pick berries, Rabbit sat alone in their lodge. After a time, Rabbit decided to wander around outside and see what could be seen.

Rabbit hopped here and there, sniffed about, ate a few plants, then arrived at Mountain Lion's home. Mountain Lion was away, so Rabbit hopped inside and hunted around to see what could be seen.

Soon Rabbit found Mountain Lion's teeth and leaped high with joy. All the animals were afraid of Mountain Lion because of the sharp teeth, but now Mountain Lion would not be able to bite them.

Clutching the teeth, Rabbit raced away to find Grandmother at home.

"Look here," Rabbit said.

Grandmother examined the teeth, nodding in approval.

"Mountain Lion will come after these teeth, so we must think of a way to hide them or that great cat will kill us."

"We must hurry," Grandmother said.

They thought hard, but they also kept close watch on the entrance to their home.

"I know," Rabbit said. "You must build a fire outside the door, put a big pot of water on to boil, then put some white stones in the water and boil them."

"That is a good start," Grandmother said.

"Mountain Lion will come and ask why you are boiling those stones. You must say I have a guest who plans to eat them."

"But you have no guest."

"I will stay inside the lodge and talk to myself. Mountain Lion will think I have a guest."

"Who is your guest?"

"My guest must be important. And powerful." Rabbit thought a moment. "I know. Chief of all the beasts."

"It is a good plan," Grandmother said.

Not long afterward, Mountain Lion tore through the bushes up to Rabbit's lodge.

"Grandmother, is Rabbit home?" Mountain Lion asked.

"Rabbit is inside with a guest."

Inside Rabbit talked loudly in two different voices, an ear cocked to Mountain Lion's words.

"What are you doing with those stones?" Mountain Lion asked.

"Rabbit's guest wants to eat them."

"Who is Rabbit's guest?"

"Chief of all the beasts."

"Yes, I know the chief well." Mountain Lion whirled around and raced away.

⊖Ϫ•ⵑ⌁⌁⌁Ϫϴ

Why Hawks Have Thin Legs

Chicken Hawk tried hard to be a great hunter, but he usually brought home little more than a mouse or some game begged off another hunter.

Out hunting one day, he admired the hunting skills of Eagle.

"Please help me kill that antelope over there," Chicken Hawk said.

"Why should I?" Eagle asked.

"You catch more than you can eat, and my family goes hungry."

"All right," Eagle said. "But I will take half the meat."

"Let us meet here at dawn," Chicken Hawk said.

Eagle agreed, so they went their separate ways.

Chicken Hawk flew home fast. Inside the family lodge, he strutted. "I shot an antelope in the head, but it did not die so I ran it into a place for the night. In the morning, I will go back and kill the animal so we will have fresh meat."

He accepted his family's praise, then slept lightly. At dawn, he flew to meet Eagle. They hunted until the sun moved halfway across the sky, then they found the antelope on a mountainside. Eagle killed it. They divided the meat, and Eagle flew away with half.

Chicken Hawk proudly carried his fresh meat to the

family lodge. "I met a poor hunter who never tasted antelope meat, so I gave him half of my kill. He promised to repay me some day."

After much praise for Chicken Hawk, the family feasted on the antelope. Afterward, they told everyone in the village about his prowess as a hunter.

When the meat was gone, a friend who learned of Chicken Hawk's hunting ability stopped by to see if it were really true.

"All true," Chicken Hawk boasted. "I brought down an antelope by myself."

His friend appeared skeptical.

"I will prove it," Chicken Hawk said. "Wait here."

He hunted hard all day long but only caught a mouse. When he brought it home, his friend refused to eat the poor game.

Chicken Hawk went out the next day but found nothing at all. Ashamed to return empty-handed, he cut meat off his own legs to take back so he would not have to admit failure to his friend.

That is why Chicken Hawks have thin legs.

Mountain Lion Tracks Coyote

One day Coyote hunted game. As the sun moved across the sky toward the west, he grew increasingly hungry. After awhile the cries of babies reached Coyote's sharp ears. He followed the sound to some rocks and discovered Mountain Lion's den. Her children lay inside, alone and defenseless. Coyote hesitated, for Mountain Lion made a powerful enemy, but Coyote was starving by now and ate them all.

Mountain Lion returned with food for her young and discovered them gone. Worried about her babies, she looked everywhere for them. Soon she found Coyote's tracks, and she knew what happened. Crying hot tears, she took off on the trail of Coyote. She tracked him long and hard, but she could not catch him.

Finally she stopped to rest beside a river and saw Rabbit nearby. "Rabbit, come here." She used a gentle voice so as not to frighten the small animal.

Rabbit froze at the sound of Mountain Lion.

"I need your help," Mountain Lion said. "Coyote is your enemy. Now he is mine because he ate my children."

Rabbit frequently lost children of her own and could sympathize. She also wanted revenge on Coyote. She hopped over to Mountain Lion and sat down.

"What can I do that you cannot?" Rabbit asked.

"I need you to help me trick Coyote."

"That I can do."

They traveled along the riverbank together until they saw a deer grazing on tall grass.

"Wait here," Mountain Lion said.

Mountain Lion stalked the deer, ran it down, then swiftly killed it.

Rabbit hopped over, and they butchered the deer.

"Rub my face with fat so no one will recognize me," Mountain Lion said.

Rabbit rubbed on the fat.

"Now put the deer on my back."

Rabbit did that too.

"Hop on my back and ride me."

Rabbit scratched a long ear in puzzlement, then threw a leg over the deer and settled on Mountain Lion's back. "Now ride me around until we find Coyote."

Rabbit whooped, and they started forward.

"This is fun, but I fail to understand how it will catch Coyote," Rabbit said.

"Wait and see."

After a time they rode onto a prairie, still looking for Coyote. Wind rustled the tall grass. Wild flowers scented the air. Yet they saw no Coyote.

Discouraged, they continued onward until they heard an animal running toward them.

"Rabbit, where did you get such a fine horse?" a voice called out.

Pretending not to hear, Rabbit rode onward.

"Rabbit, listen to me. Where did you get that fine horse?"

Still pretending not to hear, Rabbit ignored the question.

"Wait up!" The voice was closer now. "I want to see your horse."

Rabbit continued to ride.

Finally Coyote raced up. "Where did you get that horse?"

"A gift," Rabbit said.

"Get off. That fine horse is mine. I lost it and now I want it back."

"Oh no, this is my horse." Rabbit acted afraid to make Coyote more determined.

"Get off or I will eat you up," Coyote said.

Rabbit jumped off, then ran a short distance away to watch.

Coyote started to mount, but first stopped to bite fat

off the face. Too late, he recognized Mountain Lion. He turned to run, but Mountain Lion gave a mighty roar and sprang upon his back. Soon he lay dead.

Satisfied, the two mothers walked away.

Corn Mill Coyote

A woman pounded corn in a favorite corn mill made from a tree trunk. Smooth with age, it was about two feet wide and three or four feet tall. She dropped corn inside and pounded it with a pole into fine meal.

As she pounded she noticed the corn disappear faster than meal was ground. She pounded harder and faster, but she still lost more corn than she made meal. After pounding all her corn, she gathered her small portion of meal.

She waited for the next woman to pound her corn to see if the same thing happened. This woman pounded her corn but made very little meal. Now both were suspicious. They waited for the next woman. She pounded her corn, then gathered a small amount too. Now three women waited to watch the next one. This woman pounded and pounded, but the corn disappeared and little meal replaced it.

They discussed the situation, then decided something must be wrong with the corn mill. They turned the mill this way and that, and then they realized it was not the same old mill they always used.

One woman called for an axe to split the mill in half so

they could see inside. As a woman ran to get it, the mill fell on its side and rolled around on the ground. The women jumped back in astonishment.

Coyote leaped up from what had been the corn mill and ran away.

All the women laughed. Now they understood that Coyote had hidden the old corn mill and then turned into a mill to eat all their corn.

History

Deep in the dense forests, lush meadows, and sparkling streams of the Big Thicket in East Texas, the Caddo Confederacies flourished for thousands of years. They built the most influential Indian civilization in Texas.

The Lone Star State derived its name from the Caddoan language of the Hasinai, members of the Caddo Confederacies. The tribes of the Hasinai called each other *tesha*, meaning friend. The Spanish referred to them as Tejas, Texas. The French abbreviated Kadohadacho, one of the confederacies, to Caddo.

At one time the Caddo Confederacies ranged throughout the Trans-Mississippi forest that stretched from the Trinity River in Texas to the Arkansas River in Kansas. At the western edge of the Mississippian cultural complex that extended from the Carolinas deep into East Texas, the Caddo were influenced by Mesoamerican and South-western cultures.

In the ceremonial centers of their largest villages along the Red, Arkansas, Little, Quachita, and Sabine Rivers, the Caddo built huge earthen mounds as platforms for temple buildings, sacred fires, and burial chambers. They also lived near streams on isolated farms and in small villages.

From a hunting and gathering lifestyle, they created an agricultural economy. Men and women farmed corn, beans, squash, pumpkins, watermelons, and sunflower seeds in rich soil with hoes made of bone or fire-hardened walnut. Women gathered roots, nuts, and wild fruits in baskets they wove from local fibers. Men hunted deer, bears, wild hogs, quail, occasionally buffalo with bow and arrows, and they fished with trotlines.

They participated in an extensive trade network to the east and west. Many tribes exchanged a variety of items such as turquoise and copper for Caddo pottery and baskets in distinctive designs, Osage orange bows, salt, and tanned hides.

The Caddo worked together for the benefit of the community, never for the individual. They built bee-hive-shaped houses of grass and reeds about fifty feet in height and sixty feet in diameter. Inside each house a Sacred Fire continually burned in the center. Woven reed mats covered packed dirt floors, and raised beds enclosed by painted buffalo-skins hugged the walls.

In their matrilineal culture, descent of children was traced through the mother and her clan. Marriage usually occurred between people of different clans. Wives and husbands frequently separated to remarry others, but the children always remained with their mothers. Several generations of a woman's family lived together in each home.

For clothing, women dressed deer, bear, and buffalo skins. Soft deerskin was usually dyed in bright colors, decorated with small beads made of plants, and the edges cut in fringe. Men wore breechclouts, then added a buffalo-skin robe over a shoulder in winter. Women wore a poncho and skirt of deerskin, adding a fur robe in cold weather. Everyone wore soft moccasins.

They also wore earrings, bracelets, and necklaces of shells. They tattooed their bodies with elaborate designs and frequently added body paint. The men kept their hair short except for a thin braid adorned with feathers that hung from the crown of the head. Women wore their long hair in a single braid tied with a string of bright red rabbit fur.

A woman gave birth alone after building a small hut near a stream. She sank a pole in the center of the hut and clung to it during delivery. After birth, she bathed the child and her body, then returned to home and work. Later a shaman would bless and name the baby who might be nursed for five years by the mother.

The Caddo held strong religious beliefs. Ahahayo, the supreme being, created their world and rewarded good and punished evil. A *xinesi*, high priest or high priestess, communicated between the tribe and Ahahayo and kept a Sacred Fire in a temple. *Connas*, shamans, tended the people's spiritual lives, healed the sick and wounded, and conducted burials. The spirits of their dead traveled to the House of Death, presided over by Ahahayo, where they lived happy lives.

In a spirit of community, the people supported a chiefdom political system of nobles and commoners based on hereditary power. A *xinesi* governed each confederacy, and a *caddi*, assisted by *canahas*, village elders, governed each community. *Tammas*, village criers, served as police. Tribal meetings were held to decide policy. Caddos could mass thousands of warriors for a huge army, but warfare was never used for economic gain. Individuals went to war to prove valor and raise social status in raids, and the army defended Caddo Confederacies.

About 1350 a climate change in the Great Plains brought about widespread drought. The huge confederacy of chiefdoms at Spiro collapsed by 1450, and the people moved south to Red River and East Texas villages. The Caddo remained a rich and powerful people.

Lipan Apaches migrated into the Southern Plains and changed the Pueblo-Wichita-Caddo trade network. By 1500 the Wichita were supplanted by Apaches as meat-for-corn suppliers, and Caddo traders had to travel a more dangerous southern route to reach the Pueblos. An enmity developed with the Lipan.

In 1528 Cabeza de Vaca and four men survived a Spanish expedition to wash ashore near Galveston Island. They spent seven years in Texas before finally reaching Mexico.

Not long after 1542 Luis de Moscoso Alvarado, Hernando de Soto's successor, and his Spanish army attacked Caddo villages. The soldiers burned, killed, looted, then left behind several sick Spaniards. About the same time Francisco Coronado left destruction, disease, and angry Indians behind in a sweep from the west into central Kansas.

After these European contacts, diseases ran through the population of the Southeast, killing vast numbers. Indians had no natural immunities and no medicine for cures. Smallpox, measles, cholera, and other epidemics swept far ahead of sustained interaction with Europeans. By 1680 the population of the Caddo Confederacies had dropped from 200,000 to 10,000. Not only did they lose people, they lost culture through the deaths of artists, singers, dancers, priests, hunters, healers, and others. They abandoned villages, farms, ceremonial mounds, and territory.

Yet the Caddo remained strong by consolidating into three confederacies of twenty-five tribes. The Kadohadacho occupied the Great Bend of the Red River at Arkansas, Texas, and Oklahoma. The Hasinais spread across the upper reaches of the Neches and Angelina Rivers in East Texas. And the Natchitoches lived in villages on the Red River in Louisiana.

For the next one hundred and fifty years, Europeans primarily did not come back to Texas. Yet they continued to influence the Indians. In 1598 the Spanish returned to New Mexico, and soon European products slipped into the Southern Plains trade networks. The Caddo held a large trading fair at the Hasinai villages every year, and many Indian bands exchanged hides for European wares there.

Not only did the Caddo obtain metal scrapers, needles, hoes, and arrowheads, they also traded for horses. Spanish horses escaped or were raided by Apaches and Jumanos, and after the Pueblo Revolt of 1680 many more reached Indians northward across the Plains.

Horses changed the lives of Texas Indians. The animals were used to expand hunting grounds, carry riders and belongings, provide a food source if necessary, and revolutionize warfare. Foot soldiers became cavalry, and even a single rider could change the outcome of a raid or battle. As a commodity of status and wealth, the Caddo quickly made use of horses.

In 1687 Henri de Tonti went to the Caddo Confederacies to inquire into La Salle's murder by his own men. He was greeted with much ceremony by the chief of the Kadohadacho, a powerful woman whose name has been lost to history.

The Spanish decided to convert the Caddo to Christianity in 1690, but Caddos followed their own religion, and the missions were abandoned a few years later.

By the time French traders contacted the Caddo, they were able to sell horses to the surprised French. After establishing several outposts with the Natchitoches Caddos in Louisiana, the French added another outpost in 1720 at the Caddo Kadohadacho village near the Great Bend of the Red River. They sent traders to Caddos and Wichitas and established a successful trade network.

Alarmed at this, the Spanish established missions and presidios again. They wanted the Caddo to abandon their villages, live at the missions to provide manual labor, convert to Catholic Christianity, and be allies of the Spanish. In return, the Spanish would save their souls and protect them from other Indians.

The Caddo played the two European powers off each other. They traded horses and hides to the French for European products, and they provided corn and meat to the priests and soldiers for manufactured goods or raids on horses and cattle. Soon the Spanish abandoned the missions again.

In West Texas, the Lipan Apache faced a new foe in the form of Comanches riding horses down from the north. Their warfare affected Indians in East Texas. The Spanish hoped to reduce Apache and Comanche raids on

Spanish and Pueblos by limiting their trade of manufactured goods. The Indians needed arms and ammunition to compete with each other, so they turned to the French in the east. By 1750 two trade networks existed across Texas. Caddo-Wichita-Comanche traded in the north. Attakapan-Tonkawa-Apache traded across the south. They competed for the same resources, so they raided and fought each other.

France gave Louisiana to Spain in 1722 rather than lose it to Britain. Many French officials stayed at their posts in Natchitoches, so manufactured goods continued to flow into Texas and through Spanish traders too. The Caddo needed European arms more than ever, because they were being raided from the north by Osages and from the west by Choctaws.

Smallpox, measles, cholera, malaria, whooping cough, and influenza epidemics continued to decimate the Caddo population. By 1773 Caddos numbered around 2,000. As the people died, small villages combined for protection or broke apart to scatter individuals.

In 1803 the United States bought Louisiana, and the Caddo and other Texas Indians had to deal with a powerful rather than a weak government. While the Spanish wanted to trade, Anglo-Americans wanted to farm the land.

Fertile and abundant, Caddo land was easy to reach from Louisiana. Eastern Indians, trying to escape Anglo-Americans, moved into East Texas.

In 1810 the Mexican War for Independence gave the Indians of Texas relief for a decade, because Spain primarily ignored the colony while they fought the war. Euroamerican settlers left Texas for Louisiana or Mexico.

Caddos went back to planting corn, hunting deer for hides, and trying to keep out Osages, Choctaws, and other Eastern Indians.

When Mexico won independence, their new government invited Eastern Indians and Anglo-Americans to settle in Texas, hoping to control Plains Indians. These ranchers and farmers came to settle on traditional Caddo, Wichita, and Tonkawa land, and at the same time Anglo-American traders crossed Comanche and Kiowa land on the Santa Fe Trail.

By 1830 Caddos, Wichitas, Tonkawas, and other East Texas Indians were surrounded by Eastern Indians and Anglo-Americans. They all competed for the same resources, and violence escalated.

The United States in 1835 forced the Caddo in Louisiana to cede their land. Some Caddo moved to Indian Territory along with other Southeastern tribes, but most joined the Hasinai in Texas.

Texas won independence from Mexico in 1836, and the new Republic of Texas began to deal with the Indians. The Caddo and other tribes wanted peace and a boundary line between them and Anglo-Texan settlements. Yet Anglo-Texans refused to stay off tribal land, because the majority did not believe that Indians had any right to their traditional territory.

After statehood in 1845, Anglo-Texans continued to demand Indian removal or extermination. They kept pushing their settlements onto Indian land, and still powerful people like the Comanche fought back. Indian bands also fought each other, sorting out old blood revenges.

In 1846 Caddos, Wichitas, Penataka Comanches, and Tonkawas signed a peace treaty with the United States at

Council Springs, but the State of Texas refused to give up land to let the United States government make reservations for Texas Indians. After years of hostilities, in 1854 the Texas legislature finally agreed to Indian reservations. Clear Fork Reserve was set up for Penataka Comanches, and the Brazos Reserve was established for Caddos, Tonkawas, Delawares, Shawnees, and Wichita.

In 1855 Caddos settled on the 37,152-acre Brazos Reserve, a tiny area in comparison to the territory taken from them. With their homeland and spiritual sites lost, they adapted to survive. They wore Anglo-American clothes, built homes, raised cattle, hogs, chickens, continued to farm, and sent their children to school where they learned to read and write English.

But they still were not safe. In 1859 three hundred Anglo-Texans attacked the unarmed reserve tribes. They killed several Caddos. Agency personnel and troops guarding the reservation stopped the attack, but hostility toward the Indians continued to rise.

Word reached the reserves that a date had been set by Anglo-Texans to massacre all the Indians on the reservation. Caddo chief José Maria and Indian agent Robert S. Neighbors saved the 1,430 Indians, 1,050 of them Caddos, on the Brazos Reserve, as well as the Comanches on the Clear Fork Reserve. They had to leave behind most of their possessions and travel in 106-degree August heat to safely reach the Washita River in Indian Territory. When Agent Neighbors returned to Texas, he was murdered by Anglo-Texans because he helped the Indians escape.

On the Wichita and Affiliated Tribes Reservation headquartered at Fort Cobb, the Caddo now consisted of three bands: the Nadaco of the Hasinai, the Kado-hadacho, and the Hasinai. The Nadaco gave their name to the town of Anadarko, site of the Indian Agency. As Caddos struggled to rebuild their lives, Anglo-Texans still crossed deep into Indian Territory to attack them.

In 1861 Texas Indians signed a peace treaty with the Confederate States of America, but most of them wanted nothing to do with the conflict. Some Caddo bands moved to Kansas for the duration of the war. Afterward, they set about reestablishing their reservation by farming and hunting as they did in East Texas.

Fearful of losing their land again, the Wichita and Affiliated Tribes Reservation sent a delegation in 1872 to negotiate a treaty in Washington D.C. for 743,610 acres.

In 1874 the Kadohadachos and the Nadacos agreed to unite as the Caddo Indian Tribe. In 1878 the Coman-che-Kiowa Agency was moved to Anadarko and consolidated with the Wichita Agency.

During this reservation period, the Caddo experi-enced great cultural change as they adapted to survive. Christian missions opened in Anadarko to convert Indi-ans. Caddo chiefs and Comanche chief Quanah Parker founded the Native American Church in response. By 1890 the Ghost Dance, a spiritual movement that prom-ised the removal of Anglo-Americans and a return to tradition, swept through the Plains tribes. Anglo-American education systems were forced on Caddos and other Indian children, and many were sent far from home to boarding schools where they were not allowed to speak their own language.

In 1887 the United States government passed the Dawes Severalty Act, requiring the break-up of tribal land into individual allotments. Though the tribes protested, Congress allotted the Wichita and Affiliated Tribes Reservation in 1895, and 152,714 acres went to Indians while 590,896 acres went to Anglo-Americans. Caddos received an allotment of 160 acres each for 534 people.

The Caddo rebuilt their lives again, retaining as much of their heritage as possible. In 1924 the Caddo, along with other Indians, became United States citizens. In 1934 a Caddo Constitution was adopted under the Indian Reorganization Act, and in 1938 they became the Caddo Tribe of Oklahoma. In 1976 they revised their constitution.

After 1970 federal land compensation funds finally reached the Caddo, and they built the Caddo Indian Tribal Complex near Binger, Oklahoma, for the use of all their people.

Today many Caddos live and work in Caddo County, and they frequently gather at the Caddo Complex for tribal events. Each year they elect a new Caddo Tribal Princess in the spirit of their ancient matriarchy. At the traditional Murrow Dance Ground nearby, they celebrate their heritage with songs and dances such as the beloved Turkey Dance of the Caddo Confederacies.

Lipan Apache

This design is based on an Apache basket located in the
Field Museum of Natural History in Chicago.
The basket is made of yucca fibers and stitched with
green and tan yucca leaf splints.

---◆---

Myths and Legends

---◆---

Origin of the Lipan Apache

In the beginning the people lived deep down in darkness, and they knew of no other place. One day they held a council to decide if there could be another world besides their own. They agreed to send someone above to find out, but they wondered who to send on the journey. After a lengthy discussion they decided to send Wind, who consented to go.

Wind turned into a whirlwind and swirled upward to the surface of the Earth. Water covered all the land. Wind rolled back the water to expose the ground and left the water bunched to one side.

After hearing this news, the council sent Crow up to look at the exposed land. The Earth's surface was flat and looked like ashes. Crow saw many dead fish on the dry ground and started pecking out fish eyes. Soon Crow forgot all about returning to report to the council.

After a time the people wondered what happened to Crow. They still wanted news, so they sent Beaver.

Beaver noticed the water getting low and got busy building dams. One stream after another needed Beaver's help, and soon thoughts of the people faded away.

Down below in the dark the people wondered about Beaver. They still wanted news of the surface, so they sent Badger next. Badger went up, looked around, saw all was well and dry, then hurried back to tell the people.

Happy with the news, they thanked Badger for the faithful work.

The people chose four of their number to look over the world above. The four found the surface of the Earth good and decided to prepare it for habitation by the people. They chose Mirage to use in making the things of the Earth. They formed Mirage into the shape of a ball and saw beauty.

They changed the Earth using Mirage. They created mountains, hills, valleys, and lightning. They made springs with bubbling water and arroyos with rushing water.

With everything prepared, the people came up from the lower world. They were the first people, and they were animals, birds, rocks, and plants. They spoke the same language in voices as humans do today. All the varieties of animals, birds, grasses, and trees represented a different tribe.

They moved westward, following the Sun around the Earth. They came to a stream. Willow, green and gray to stand for young and old, stopped and decided to live there.

Later Alligator-Bark Juniper, wearing turquoise beads, stopped, and the beads became blue berries.

Juniper, adorned with red beads, stayed near a group of hills, and the beads turned to red berries.

Wearing a necklace of black beads, Oak spread deep roots near a lake, and the black beads turned to acorns.

In the shade of a mountain, Chokecherry's red beads turned to red berries.

The people moved onward, but they never paused. Finally they decided to rest. Someone placed a white walking cane over them, and they slept one night.

When they awoke the next morning, the Moon and the Sun took the lead.

"Nothing will disturb you," the Moon and the Sun said. "Everything ahead is good for you. We will never stop no matter what happens on Earth. We will always keep going."

The people resumed their journey, following the path of the Sun. The second people, humans, chose places to live. The western people, perhaps the Chiricahua, stopped first. As various people found a land they liked, they stayed and became different tribes with different languages.

Finally the Tonkawa stopped and then the Lipan, who were the very last to find a home. And the people were all in place upon the Earth.

Changing Woman Gives Birth to Killer-of-Enemies

Changing Woman took great pleasure in giving birth to her children, but she worried about them. No matter how hard she tried to keep them safe, Big Owl, a giant monster, would see their footprints in the ground around her home. He would hide in the tall grass, then snatch and gobble them right up.

One day Changing Woman lay down in the soft grass outside her home, wanting another baby. Rain fell from the sky and entered her body. Soon she grew large with child, and she knew this one would be a great person. In four days, she gave birth to a son. She vowed to find a way to keep him safe.

She dug a trench under the place of fire, then put her son down there. When Big Owl came to call, he saw no new child and left in disappointment. She raised her son in the trench and kept him safe, but sometimes he went outside to play.

Big Owl came to visit again and saw small tracks in the ground. He knew Changing Woman had a new child, and he wanted to eat this one too. Yet he could not find the young one anywhere.

Later Big Owl came back and saw the boy playing outside. Now he really felt hungry, but he had to think of some trick to get the child so he went away again.

Changing Woman watched her son grow strong, but she still worried about his safety. She knew he needed to be able to kill anything that came to fight him. She made a small bow and arrows for him, then taught him how to use them.

When Big Owl returned, he saw that the boy was taller and stronger. "I want that boy," he said.

"No. He is not for you," Changing Woman said. "I got him from the rain. He is Thunder's boy, so you must not touch him."

Now this news made Big Owl angry, but it also made him afraid. He did not want to challenge Thunder, so he went away and left the boy to grow into a man who came to be called Killer-of-Enemies.

Killer-of-Enemies Slays Monsters

As Changing Woman predicted, her son grew up to be a great man of the people. After killing many monsters, he earned the name Killer-of-Enemies.

The first monster he killed was Buffalo. One day his mother told him about Buffalo, a monster who killed the people when they tried to get close. He vowed to deal with Buffalo.

He saw Buffalo far out on the plains lying under a mesquite tree. No one could sneak up on Buffalo because of the flat land, so Killer-of-Enemies decided to ask for help. He prayed, for one was never too strong to ask for help. He called on Gopher.

Gopher popped up from a hole.

"See Buffalo down there." Killer-of-Enemies pointed toward the mesquite tree.

"Yes," Gopher said.

"I want to kill Buffalo for the people. I need your help. Are you able?"

Gopher thought it over. "Yes, I will help you. Wait here."

While Killer-of-Enemies waited Gopher dug four trenches, one after another, and then a hole right up to Buffalo. Gopher tugged at Buffalo's elbow, pulling the hair.

Buffalo snorted and looked down. "What do you want?"

"I need some of your fur," Gopher said. "My children are cold, and it will warm them. Lie still so I may take it."

Buffalo snorted again but lay still.

Gopher plucked at the fur until a round area under the elbow revealed the beating of Buffalo's heart.

"Thank you." Gopher hurried back to Killer-of-Enemies. "Shoot for Buffalo's heart, then run to the fourth trench."

Killer-of-Enemies walked across the plains until he had Buffalo in range, then he notched an arrow and raised his bow. He released the arrow to fly straight toward the hairless round area and deep into Buffalo's heart.

Buffalo bellowed and staggered up, shaking a shaggy head. Killer-of-Enemies ran away, but he was no match for Buffalo. The monster dug at the first trench, but Killer-of-Enemies was already through and racing toward the next one. Buffalo ripped up each trench with sharp hooves until arriving at the fourth where Killer-of-Enemies lay hidden. Bellowing again, Buffalo lowered sharp horns, then fell over dead.

Killer-of-Enemies jumped up, gave a cry, and danced around Buffalo. "This is the end of your killing the people. You are now different. When the people need anything from you, you must help them. Flesh, skin, fur, even bone. You will be useful to the people."

No longer a monster or huge in size, Buffalo raised a shaggy head. "I agree, but people must not be wasteful or careless of my body. If they ever misuse my meat or skin, I will get revenge on the hunter."

"Hunters will be careful how they use you and show you respect."

Killer-of-Enemies returned to his mother. "Buffalo will no longer harm the people. I killed the monster."

"You did well, but there is another monster hurting the people. This one is fierce and very hard to get."

"I am a fierce one. I am hard to get. What is this monster's name?"

"Antelope."

Killer-of-Enemies tracked Antelope to a mesquite tree on the plains. The monster stood in the shade, and no one could get near.

Realizing he needed help, Killer-of-Enemies turned to Sotol Stalk. "Are you good for anything? Can you be of help to me?"

"Yes," Sotol Stalk said. "I will help any way I can."

Killer-of-Enemies made four arrows of Sotol Stalk. He made one each of black, blue, yellow, and white.

He turned back to Antelope, who still rested in the shade of the mesquite tree.

Killer-of-Enemies shot the black arrow to the east. Black smoke rose from the ground. Antelope raced over there as quickly as possible, then returned to the tree.

Killer-of-Enemies shot a blue arrow to the south. Blue smoke rose from the ground. Antelope ran over there, then returned more slowly to the tree.

Killer-of-Enemies shot a yellow arrow to the west. Yellow smoke rose from the ground. Antelope trotted over there and then limped back with tongue hanging out.

Killer-of-Enemies shot a white arrow to the north. White smoke rose from the ground. Antelope stumbled over there, then staggered back to the mesquite tree.

Holding his war club high, Killer-of-Enemies walked up and struck the monster's forehead. Antelope fell dead.

"You are no longer a monster," Killer-of-Enemies said. "From now on the people will use your skin, flesh, and all parts of your body."

Antelope looked up. "I agree only if you give people a rule first. They must not mix fur and meat. They must use them separately to stay clean."

"They will do so."

Killer-of-Enemies returned to his mother. "Antelope is no longer a monster. I killed that one."

"You did well," Changing Woman said. "Yet there is another monster. No one has ever been able to harm this dangerous one."

"What is the monster's name?"

"Eagle."

Killer-of-Enemies journeyed far in search of Eagle. Finally he saw four eagles perched on top of a smooth rocky cliff, a mother, father, and two young ones. He did not know how to get up there, so he walked around the cliff trying to find footholds.

An old horse stood near the base of the cliff, munching dry grass.

"Are you good for anything?" Killer-of-Enemies asked. "I need help."

"Yes, I am good for many things. I can help any way you want."

"I want your entrails."

Horse pulled out entrails.

Killer-of-Enemies wrapped them around his body until he was covered. He walked out to an open area so he could be seen from above.

Father Eagle swooped down and picked up Killer-of-Enemies by the head, then carried him back to his nest. He set Killer-of-Enemies before his two children.

"Eat," Father Eagle said. "This is your food."

"Shush," Killer-of-Enemies said when the young eagles started to eat.

The young eagles stepped back. "Father, we are afraid. When we try to take a bite, our food goes 'shush.'"

Father Eagle reached for the food's heart and squeezed hard with his talons, but he did not touch more than the entrails. "Now eat. That sound is air coming out. I must go hunt."

Mother Eagle and Father Eagle flew away together.

Killer-of-Enemies stood up. "When your father comes home, where does he sit?"

"When heavy rain falls, he perches on the point of rock to the east," the young eagles said.

Killer-of-Enemies went to the point of rock and patiently waited.

When rain began to fall, Father Eagle flew back with a roaring noise like a whirlwind. As he slowed, flapping his wings to land facing the east, he touched the rock with his talons. As he started to close his wide wings, Killer-of-Enemies leaped out and hit him on the head with his war club. Father Eagle fell off the rock dead.

Killer-of-Enemies walked back to the nest. "When will your mother return, and where will she sit?"

"She comes when heavy rain falls and sits to the west," the young eagles said.

Soon the rain fell again, so Killer-of-Enemies hid on the west side of the rock. When he heard the sound of wings beating like a strong wind, he clutched his war club. Mother Eagle settled downward on the rock, but just as she closed her wings he hit her on the head and knocked her off the rock dead.

He returned to the nest. "Which of you flies all the way to the ground?"

"I get halfway before I fall," the youngest said.

"I nearly reach the bottom before I fall."

Killer-of-Enemies threw the youngest over the edge of the rock, then climbed on the back of the other one. "Fly downward and do not drop me."

The young eagle flew down, then he began to fall near

the bottom. When they finally set down, Killer-of-Enemies killed this young eagle. He turned to the youngest, who lay on the ground.

"Eagles are no longer monsters. None will grow larger than you."

The young eagle stared in wonder.

"I give you this rule. People will highly respect you, but you must help them. They will use your feathers in ceremonies and in prayer, but they must mention your name."

He plucked one feather from Father Eagle, then blew it upward. "This is a bird of a certain name." A bird flew up, chirping and singing. Soon he created all the birds, one after another.

Killer-of-Enemies returned to his mother. "Eagle is dead. I killed the big monster."

"You did well," Changing Woman said. "There is another monster bird. This one destroys with powerful eyes. No one may approach for fear of being seen and killed."

"I am powerful too," he said. "What is the name of this monster?"

"Owl."

Killer-of-Enemies searched long and hard until he found Owl's home. He tried to get close, but Owl kept hopping out and looking in every direction. He walked around Owl's home, wondering how he could get near. He saw a small gray lizard.

"Are you of any use to people?" he asked.

"Yes," Lizard said. "I can be of help to those who wish it."

"I need your help." Killer-of-Enemies explained his mission.

Lizard thought a moment. "Owl only kills from a distance. If you get close, you are safe."

"That is good to know."

"Watch me. You must do as I do. I will make a path for you to Owl's home. I will stop three times and raise my head each time. The fourth time I will be at Owl's home."

Killer-of-Enemies watched Lizard make a path to Owl's home. When Lizard returned, Killer-of-Enemies followed the path exactly. When he stopped the fourth time, he stood at the entrance to Owl's home so he stepped inside to look around.

Owl saw him and blinked in astonishment. "I check outside all the time. What type of eyes do I have that would not see you?"

Killer-of-Enemies moved closer.

Owl grew more agitated. "I believed I had a powerful eye, but you are right in my home with my family."

"I will tell you the story of how I came to be here." Killer-of-Enemies held out a piece of buffalo intestine. "You can eat this while I talk." He tossed the meat on the fire to cook. "Gather around."

Owl's family drew close.

"Watch me."

They turned their faces so large eyes clearly saw him.

He grabbed the hot intestine, then hit them all across the eyes with it. They fell over dead.

"Your power is taken away from you. You will never be big again." he said. "This is my rule. From now on the people will use your feathers when they make a ceremony, and they will make good use of you."

Killer-of-Enemies returned to his mother. "I killed Owl. That monster will no longer hurt the people."

"You did well," Changing Woman said. "That is the last of the monsters."

$\forall \dot{x}_\bullet {}^\prime \mathord{\sim}\mathord{\sim}\mathord{\sim} \dot{x}\,\forall$

Changing Woman Regains Wise One

After Changing Woman gave birth to Killer-of-Enemies, she brought forth a twin called Wise One. She hid her second son in a pool of water to keep him safe. Killer-of-Enemies was raised under the fire while Wise One was brought up in the water.

After a time she wanted to get her sons together, but she did not know how to do it. She made a special bow and arrows for Killer-of-Enemies, and one evening he came home without them. She wondered what happened to them, but he refused to tell her. She made him a bow and arrows two more times, and he returned without them.

After the fourth time, she shook her head. "You must tell me about losing your bows and arrows."

"I go down to the water's edge, and I play arrow shooting games with my younger brother. He wins them all."

"I am glad you found your brother. He is smart. You are strong. I am your mother. We should all live together here in my home."

Killer-of-Enemies nodded in agreement. "Wise One likes to live in the water."

"He knows nothing else. We must bring him here."

"How can we do this?"

"Go play with him. When he gets out of the water, grab his hair and call for me."

Killer-of-Enemies went back to the pool of water, wearing rawhide clothes.

"Why are you wearing those clothes?" Wise One asked.

"They protect my skin if I roll on the ground."

Wise One lost interest, and they started to play. They shot arrows from the edge of the bank, then farther and farther away from the water. When Killer-of-Enemies decided the time was right, he grabbed his brother by the hair. Wise One bit him on the arm, but the rawhide protected his skin. Killer-of-Enemies held on tightly to Wise One as he called his mother.

Changing Woman hurried to get her son, and she took him home. They lived happily together, and the boys played shooting-arrows.

One day she warned them not to play near a particular pool of water because Turtle, a dangerous one, lived deep in its depths. If one drop of water touched them, they would have to go into the pond with Turtle.

Soon they set out for Turtle's pond, but they found only a pretty blue pool that did not look dangerous. They played along the bank, forgetting about Turtle.

At the noise, Turtle's head popped out of the water. The boys remembered their mother's warning and stepped back. Turtle saw them and came out of the pond. They retreated, but Turtle followed them.

Killer-of-Enemies grew brave. He put a forefinger on Turtle's shell, but he got stuck.

Turtle headed for the water, dragging Killer-of-Enemies. Wise One ran alongside, trying to pull his brother free. At the last moment, Killer-of-Enemies licked his other hand. Turtle had to let go and slide into the water alone.

The boys thought this great fun. They played with Turtle, getting stuck and riding the hard shell to the water's edge before licking a hand and jumping free. After a time Turtle was too exhausted from all their tricks to crawl or carry anything.

They picked up Turtle and walked away from the pool of water. The farther they went on dry land, the more water ran out of the pond until finally it dried out. Playing, they turned Turtle upside down to spin round and round. When they grew tired, they left Turtle under a juniper tree and went home to rest.

"What did you do today?" Changing Woman asked.

"We played with Turtle," Wise One said.

"Turtle is not dangerous at all," Killer-of-Enemies said.

"We left Turtle not far from here," Wise One said.

"Oh no!" Changing Woman said. "You must return Turtle right now, or there will be no water."

The boys went back and tossed Turtle into the empty pond. Water bubbled up from the ground and refilled the pool with water.

They went home to their mother, no longer afraid of Turtle.

"Turtle is back in the water," Killer-of-Enemies said.

"That is good, but I must warn you of another dangerous one," Changing Woman said.

"What is it?" Killer-of-Enemies asked.

"Where is it?" Wise One asked.

"Never go near the prickly pear cactus close to the coast." Changing Woman drew them close. "Before you go out to play again, I will make you new arrows."

Soon Killer-of-Enemies had four new arrows. The first had one feather, the second had two feathers, the third had three feathers, and the fourth had four feathers.

Despite their mother's warning, the boys headed for the prickly pear cactus place on the coast. They played shooting-arrows on the way and soon they arrived.

They tried to pick a few prickly pears, but big waves kept washing up and sweeping them backward. Frustrated, they could not get close to the cactus.

Killer-of-Enemies thought about the situation, then he set his first arrow deep into the ground near the cactus. He picked one of the pears. A big wave came up, but it stopped at the arrow.

He stuck the second arrow into the sand, then raced ahead of the water to pick another cactus. The water almost caught him, but it stopped at the second arrow.

Wise One wanted a pear, so he helped his brother push the third arrow into the ground. They picked fruit, then ran. The water rushed up and almost caught them, but it stopped at the third arrow.

Finally Killer-of-Enemies stuck the fourth arrow into the ground. They ran forward to pick pears. The water sprayed upward into a great fountain and fell toward them. They ran hard to the fourth arrow, and it stopped the water.

After four arrows the water failed, so they were no longer afraid. They picked all the fruit from the cactus, cleaned off the spines, and carried it home to their mother.

"Here is the prickly pear fruit," Killer-of-Enemies said.

"No danger to us," Wise Boy added.

Changing Woman bit into a juicy pear. "You have

done well, but there might be other monsters, other dangers for you to change for our people."

Killer-of-Enemies and Wise One looked into each other's eyes and nodded in anticipation.

Killer-of-Enemies Teaches Raid and Warfare

After killing all the monsters, Killer-of-Enemies made rules for the people. He also started all the work they must do. The arrow making, the raiding, the war, and the other things that were done began with him.

He left his home in the Guadalupe Mountains and went out on a raid. Soon he brought back many horses, which he turned loose at a place called Blue-Stem-Grass-Whitens. Next he made ready to go after his enemy. He selected a bow, a quiver full of arrows, a war club, a spear, and a shield. He picked the fastest horse. He met the enemy, fought, and won.

On the way home, he left his hoop and pole. They are there today, petrified. His spear, shield, bow and arrows, and war club are on that bluff too. He put his horses to pasture, and they became the black weeds and bushes at Blue-Stem-Grass-Whitens.

When he reached home, he tossed scalps at the feet of his mother to prove his success as he had done many times before.

"My work here is done," he said. "A new generation of the people comes, and they must do as I did. They must follow my way and my rules."

"They will do as they must do," Changing Woman said. "You have accomplished all the tasks set for you, and now it is time for us to go."

Killer-of-Enemies left with his mother for their home in a place that is not known, although some say they still live in the Guadalupe Mountains with Wise One.

Prairie Dogs Save a Woman

A Lipan woman escaped from the Comanche and headed toward her home in the mountains. She shivered in the cold wind that blew down from the north, for she had run away with no food or buffalo robe, only a ragged hide blanket. She walked hard and fast to keep warm and to cover distance.

Storm clouds rolled across the sky, obscuring the warm rays of sunlight. Soon rain fell, then snow. She walked faster, but the plains stretched out endlessly toward the mountains. Despair filled her.

As the day grew even darker at sunset, she came to a prairie dog town. Ice pelted her as she stumbled across several holes and collapsed in the middle of the town. She shivered under the hide and felt the cold drive deep into her bones. She feared she had exchanged one death for another.

Alone in her misery, she noticed light glowing from a nearby prairie dog hole. She crawled close to the hole and looked down. Prairie dog people sat around a cozy fire. She needed their help, but she could not reach them. She crouched beside the hole, shaking from the cold.

Young Prairie Dog looked up and saw her. "A woman sits outside our hole. Do you think she is going to the mountains?"

"She is no concern of ours," Father Prairie Dog said, warming his feet by the fire.

"The mountains are far away," Young Prairie Dog said.

"For a two-legged, they are," Father Prairie Dog agreed.

"She looks cold," Young Prairie Dog said.

"That is because she grows no fur coat," Father Prairie Dog said.

"She looks hungry," Young Prairie Dog said.

Mother Prairie Dog glanced up. "Maybe we should help her."

"I would not like to live without my warm fur coat," Young Prairie Dog said.

"My husband," Mother Prairie Dog said. "Will you go out and call her in here?"

"No. She may be trouble," Father Prairie Dog said. "If you want to help her, you go."

Young Prairie Dog ran up the hole and poked out a head. "Come inside."

"How can I?" the woman asked. "The hole is small and I am large."

"Try. We have plenty of room." Young Prairie Dog dropped down into the hole.

"I will try." She pulled at the hole with her hands, and it seemed to grow. She pulled harder, then she put her head into the hole. Encouraged, she lowered her entire body into the hole. She stood up and looked around. The campfire appeared far away. Surprised at the large size of the hole, she walked to the fire and sat down with the prairie dog family.

"Thank you for letting me come into your home," she said. "Comanches captured me, but I escaped. I am trying to reach my home in the mountains."

"Warm your hands over the fire," Mother Prairie Dog said."

"Could I take some of this fire with me to keep warm on my journey?"

"No," Father Prairie Dog said. "This is prairie dog fire and no one may take it away."

"Are you hungry?" Young Prairie Dog asked.

"Yes. I am weak from hunger."

Mother Prairie Dog rubbed her hand on the wall, and a small piece of meat fell off. She rubbed her hand again, and a small piece of fat came off. She rubbed her hand a third time, and a small piece of dried yucca fruit came into her hand. When she rubbed her hand a fourth time, a little honey from sotol stalk came into her hand.

She gave all this to the hungry woman. "These four are more than enough for you. As long as you stay in this hole, you will not be able to eat them all."

Surprised, the woman ate the food, then ate more. No matter how much she ate, she always had more. When she felt completely full, she still had more food.

After several days, Father Prairie Dog went up the hole to see if snow still covered the ground. It did. Each day he checked until it was mostly gone.

"You should go now," Father Prairie Dog said to the woman. "Your smell is different from prairie dogs and it bothers my children."

"My poor clothes will not keep me warm," the woman said.

Father Prairie Dog nodded. "I will give you no ceremony or power because when the children of your people grow big, they are given bows and arrows to shoot prairie dogs. We do not like that, so we will not help you in that way."

"I understand," she said.

Father Prairie Dog pulled grama grass from his nest, crushed it until soft, and gave it to her. "Put this under your armpits, and it will keep you warm on your journey. When you see the camp of your people, leave it on a flat rock. Someone will bring it back to me."

She did as he instructed, then she saw a small clay cup of water. She decided she should drink it before she left, so she drank all the water. When she set the cup down, it was full again.

"Take the food I gave you on your journey," Mother Prairie Dog said. "When you see the camp of your people, put it on top of a flat rock and leave it behind. Someone will bring it back to me."

"Thank you for your help." The woman started up the hole to the top.

"Travel safe," Young Prairie Dog called.

Once on the surface, she started toward the mountains again. She felt no cold although a bitter wind howled down from the north. She walked, then rested and ate. She felt no thirst. She walked, then ate more. No matter how much she ate, she always had plenty.

Finally she came to the mountains. She could see her people's camp in the distance. She set the food on top of a flat rock, then she set the grama grass beside it.

She reached her camp to much joyful reunion, but she told no one about the prairie dogs. She waited, hoping to receive a vision of power from Prairie Dog. None came to her. After a time, she told her people the amazing story of her visit in a prairie dog hole.

Horse Ceremony

A man went out on the flats to catch horses. He saw four fine animals. The black faced west. The blue, or gray, faced south. The yellow, or sorrel, faced east. And the white faced north.

He wanted those horses. Yet they would be difficult to catch. They stood in the open and could easily run away if he moved close. He thought about the situation, then came to a decision.

"Give me rain," he said.

Rain poured from the sky.

The black horse shook hard and the rain stopped.

"Give me rain," he said.

Rain poured from the sky.

The gray horse shook hard and the rain stopped.

"Give me rain," he said.

Rain poured from the sky.

The sorrel horse shook hard and the rain stopped.

"Give me rain," he said.

Rain poured from the sky.

The white horse shook hard and the rain stopped.

"Give me rain," he said.

Rain poured from the sky a fifth time.

He walked over and stood in front of the horses.

"Grandchild," the black horse said. "I have looked

long and hard for people, but I saw no one. Now you stand before me and you are a man. If you know about horses, you may have us. If you have no power, we will not belong to you."

The man stood still, holding horsehair ropes of black, blue, yellow, and white.

The black horse shook hard. A ball of white clay and black-tipped feathers of the eagle fell and scattered across the ground.

The man shook hard, and white clay and black-tipped feathers of the eagle fell from him.

He walked up to the black horse and slipped on the black rope. He staked it to the ground.

The blue horse shook hard, and blue paint and blue-tipped feathers of the eagle fell to the ground. The man did the same, then used his blue rope to stake the horse to the ground.

The yellow horse shook hard, and yellow ochre and yellow-tipped feathers of the eagle fell to the ground. The man did the same, then used his yellow rope to stake the horse to the ground.

The white horse shook hard, and white clay and white-tipped feathers of the eagle fell to the ground. The man did the same, then used his white rope to stake the horse to the ground.

"Grandchild," the horses said. "You know our ways, so we belong to you now."

Wind and Thunder Quarrel

"On this green Earth, I keep all in order," Wind said. "I do every bit of the work."

"No," Thunder said. "I keep this world in proper shape. I do the work."

"My power is greatest." Wind blew hard, scattering leaves and twigs to prove the point.

"The Earth needs me." Thunder grew angry.

"Not so much as me."

"Prove it." Thunder rumbled away into the distance, refusing to remain around Wind any longer.

Wind howled for a moment at being left alone, then thought better of it. "I can work by myself. I keep all in order anyway. I make the plants grow."

To prove this, Wind began to blow. And blow. And blow. Yet no plants grew. Earth slowly turned from green to brown, parched by the wind and lack of rain.

Finally Wind admitted that those hastily spoken words were not true. Earth needed Thunder.

Wind went to Thunder. "I cannot do this alone. Earth needs us both. Together. I want you to work with me again."

Thunder rumbled in agreement, then louder and louder. Soon rain fell on Earth. Plants turned green with new growth.

Wind followed Thunder, happy to rustle the stalks of tall grass again.

From that moment onward, Thunder and Wind worked together to take care of the Earth.

Rescue by the Dead

One day the people broke camp to find a new site. While parents packed belongings, children raced here and there on horseback, playing games with each other.

A young girl mounted her favorite pony by stepping onto a log since she was too short to use a stirrup. Once atop the horse, she rode as easily as the others. Laughing and shouting, she continued to play when the group left camp and started down a trail.

Sometime later she rode off the trail, then realized she was separated from the others. She grew confused and frightened. She tried to find them, but she was lost.

Clouds blew in from the north and covered the sky. Soon rain fell, pounding harder until she was wet all over. She opened her parfleche and took out her doll, then rode under a tree for shelter. She dismounted so she could hug the tree trunk, but rain still pelted down on her.

As her horse wandered away, she realized she had forgotten to ground-tie her mount. Now she was alone, wet, and night crept close. Frightened, she clung to her doll and then started to run. Lightning flashed through the sky and thunder crashed nearby. She cried out, stumbling over uneven ground.

A man leaped out in front of her.

"Father," she gasped. "You are dead."

"I knew the power of lightning when I lived with you, so I rode it to your side." He reached out to her. "Why do you cry?"

"I lost my people on the trail. I am frightened."

"Dry your tears, little one. I will take you to my mother, your loving grandmother."

He knelt so she could climb onto his back, then he

started to walk.

"This is not the way to my people, is it?" she asked.

"No. We are going to the camps where my mother lives."

As they neared the large encampment, he covered her face with soft deerskin. "Do not look around us."

She did as he bid, for she was still afraid.

Inside his mother's tepee, he set his daughter on the ground. "I found a lost child. She does not belong with us yet, so I will take her back to her mother."

"How are you, child?" Grandmother asked.

"Better now." She could hear children playing outside and turned toward the sound.

"Do not go outside and play," Father said.

"Yes. Go out and play with them," Grandmother said.

"No." Father shook his head. "If you do, you will never see your mother again."

Outside the children called for her to come and play. They laughed, naming all the games they could play together.

Father covered all the holes in the tepee, then he built up dirt around the edges so the children could not peep inside to see her.

She watched all this, hugging her doll close.

"You must stay inside," Father said. "Play with your doll. She looks like you."

She stayed in the tepee.

Time passed but she could not tell how long because she could not see night or day. She played with her doll and listened to the children outside.

"These dead people will move camp soon because they follow the live people," Father said. "The dead stay close even though the living cannot see them. When we are near, I will take you to your mother."

Soon the camps of the dead moved, following the live people.

Father put her on the back of Grandmother and covered her face. "Do not look at the dead, or you will never see your mother again," he said.

She nodded, clinging to Grandmother's back.

After a time, they camped. In the morning, Father covered her face, then put her on his back. He walked through the camps of the dead to a ridge. On the other side the living camped beside a stream that ran toward the west.

Father set her down on the ground. "I would like to take you all the way to your people, but I cannot do that. If we were seen together, I would have to take you back to the dead."

They walked to the top of a hill, then stopped.

"Walk to the other side and follow the stream," he said. "Four people are ahead. They are dead."

"Will they hurt me?"

"They spy on live people. Do not let them frighten you. When you reach the water, step into it wearing your clothes. Wash your body, even inside your ears. You must wash your clothes too, for they have been in the land of the dead. You must leave your doll behind since she has seen the dead."

"Yes, Father."

He smiled at her. "When you reach the two hills where the people drive the horses through, you will meet someone. Do not be afraid. No harm will come to you between here and the camps. And when you get home, tell the people your story."

She gazed at him for a moment, then he nudged her

forward. "Go. You belong with the living now."

She trudged ahead, glancing back as she passed the top of the hill. She saw only a streak of lightning in the clear blue sky.

Near the stream she caught sight of four quail with their mouths wide open as they headed away from the camps. She had seen quail near their camps before, only now she knew them for the scouts of dead people.

When she came to the stream, she hugged her doll before hiding her under some rocks. She waded into the water, then washed her body and clothes. She stretched her deerskin dress until it was soft again, then she slipped it over her head and started for the camps.

She followed the trail between the hills and saw a man on horseback.

"Is that you, our lost one?" he called.

"Yes. I am coming home."

He lifted her up high to the horse's back, and they rode into the camps right up to her mother's tepee.

"Here is your child," the man called. "She has returned to you."

A woman ran outside. Tears running down her cheeks, she held out her arms.

"Where have you been, my daughter?"

"Father saved me."

"How can that be?"

"He lives with the dead, but he sent me back. I could not stay because nothing killed me. He said that when I am very old and have only a few black hairs among the silver, then I will return to him. Now I am with you."

"But how did he find you?"

"It started with lighting, and I will tell everyone my story around the campfire tonight."

Coyote Takes Buffalo Away from Crow

Coyote arrived at a big camp of the people. They played games, including hoop and pole, but they did not have enough food for a good feast.

Thinking about how to solve the problem, Coyote saw Crow glide down from the sky and land nearby to scout the area. Crow lifted an arrow quiver from his back, but he tipped it by mistake. Arrows and a large piece of buffalo intestine fell out. Crow quickly put them back in the quiver, then took to the sky. He flew in ever widening circles above the camp.

The people watched because they saw the piece of meat. They were hungry. If Crow had food, they wanted some too. They watched to see where Crow flew, but only Bat, known for sharp eyesight, kept Crow in view as the black bird flew out of the area. Bat told the people Crow's last direction.

They quickly packed up camp, then they started after Crow.

Soon they arrived at Crow's home near a grassy hill. They expected to find fresh meat, but they found only the ashes of a dead fire. Disappointment filled them, for they had been sure Crow was the only one who ate meat all the time.

They camped near Crow's place and looked around for signs of fresh meat. They found none. They tried to learn more about Crow, but they discovered nothing new. Finally they called a council and discussed how to get food from Crow.

Coyote listened to the council for a while, then decided to help. "Crow is suspicious of you."

Not a single one of the people disagreed.

"If you go away and leave me here, I might be able to get you food."

Everyone decided that if it could be done, tricky Coyote was the one to do it.

"You must pick off all my fur and make me look like a hairless dog."

They set right to work, leaving only a little hair on the tail. They gave Coyote obsidian claws and balls of obsidian for eyes.

"Now you must leave me under that old bedding," Coyote said. "When Crow flies away, the children will come out and find me. Maybe I will learn something."

They did as Coyote asked and then left the area.

Coyote lay there until the young crows came out to play. Only the youngest saw Coyote.

"Look here!" Young Crow drug Coyote out from under the brush bedding. "I want this little dog."

Young Crow pulled Coyote home and got into trouble.

"Get rid of that animal," a brother said. "That dog may be a trick."

"No. I want to keep it," Young Crow said.

"If you must keep it, light a stick and put the fire to its nails," a sister said. "If it stays still, that means it is gentle. If it jerks, it cannot be trusted and must be killed."

Coyote did not like the sound of this, but he stayed still like a gentle dog.

"You must also light a stick and poke it into the dog's eye," another brother said. "If it does not close its eye, it is a gentle dog and will do no harm."

Coyote liked this idea even less, but he remained gentle.

Young Crow agreed, so they lit two sticks. They thrust one into Coyote's eye and watched for a reaction. No movement. They put the other to Coyote's nails and waited again. Still no movement.

"This is a gentle dog," Young Crow said.

The others agreed, so they let Coyote loose to run around camp. Crow came home that night, then he got out a big pipe and filled it with tobacco. Crow prayed with the children, asking for buffalo. Now Coyote knew Crow had fresh meat hidden somewhere.

Later that night Crow carried the pipe to a nearby grassy hill. Coyote watched. Crow prayed again, then a doorway opened into buffalo country. Old and young buffalo of all types lived there. Coyote knew that many herds of game lived in underground homes kept by caretakers, and it was why game sometimes grew scarce.

Crow went inside the cave and walked among the buffalo. Crow held the bowl of the pipe and extended the stem outward. When a buffalo came forward for a puff, that one was led outside with the pipe. Crow killed the buffalo, and the family started using the meat.

Coyote stayed many days to learn how to get the buffalo out for the people. When Crow prayed for another buffalo, Coyote watched and listened. By the fourth time, Coyote knew where Crow kept the sacred pipe and tobacco as well as what ceremonial words to speak.

At last Coyote took some tobacco and placed it in his ear. He stole the pipe next, filled the bowl with tobacco, then prayed for the buffalo. He went to the grassy hill and prayed again. He opened the buffalo home and saw the herd way in back.

Coyote walked among them, holding out the pipe. "Do you want to come out and see the beautiful land?"

The buffalo thought about the question.

Coyote held out the pipe to a shaggy buffalo. "Take it

and be free."

The buffalo took the pipe and followed Coyote out of the cave. The others ran after them, raising clouds of dust. Not one buffalo stayed behind.

Coyote raced ahead of the big herd. "Hurry! You must go as far as you can go."

After a time Coyote grew tired. He grabbed the lead buffalo by the chest and hung on there. Coyote guided the herd toward the camps of the people. When the herd arrived, Coyote leaped to the ground. The people killed some of the buffalo, but most of the herd ran onward.

After Coyote rode on the buffalo, the chest hair on them all turned whitish as it is today.

At the grassy hill, Crow discovered the buffalo gone and turned in anger to the children. "We lost our food because you kept that dog. We had an easy time with our game right at the door, but now times will be hard."

Young Crow cried in remorse, missing the dog and the buffalo.

Crow flew to the camps of the people and watched them butcher buffalo. They were no longer hungry or needy.

"You took my buffalo," Crow said. "Now I ask only that you leave me a little fat from between the ribs and some fat from the eye socket."

The people agreed, so Lipan buffalo hunters always left the eyes and some fat from the ribs for Crow.

Coyote and Wildcat Compare Claws

"Today I will visit Wildcat," Coyote said. "That rascal is always fun."

Coyote arrived at Wildcat's den and lay down. "I want to have a chat."

Wildcat yawned, showing sharp teeth.

Unimpressed, Coyote looked at Wildcat's paws. "You have fine paws." Coyote raised one and felt of it. "This is soft and spongy."

Wildcat nodded.

"Look at mine." Coyote raised a paw. "It is rough and hard. Let us scratch each other."

"That is not fair. Look. I have no claws. You will get the better of me."

"No. This is just for fun. You scratch me, and I will scratch you."

"No. You have big, hard claws, and I have none at all. You want to get the better of me."

"Not me," Coyote said. "This is for fun."

"Are you sure?"

"Yes, indeed."

"I agree then. Where will we start?" Wildcat held up a paw. "On a leg?"

"No. Our backs. You first."

"You go first."

They argued for some time before Coyote finally agreed to scratch first.

Wildcat lay down, then Coyote scratched long and hard. Wildcat squirmed and complained as if it really hurt, but only a little fur came out and the scratch was not deep.

Next Coyote lay down. Wildcat stood up, shot out

long, sharp claws, and raked them down Coyote's back to pull out flesh and fur.

Coyote growled.

Wildcat retracted claws, then placed fur and flesh in front of Coyote.

"I do not understand," Coyote said. "How did you do that? You have no claws, so you must have used a sharp rock on me."

"Look." Wildcat shot out claws. "You want to scratch again?"

"You fooled me." Coyote ran off to think up a better plan to get the best of Wildcat.

A Fearless Young Man

A band of Lipan moved to a new place where they wanted to stay and put up their tepees.

A young man hardly more than a skinny boy lay soundly asleep on top of a tepee cover, dreaming of fighting monsters.

"Wake up!" his grandmother said. "I want to put up that cover."

He jerked awake and looked about for monsters.

"Go see why that crowd gathers." She knew he would fight anything. "Trouble, I bet."

He jumped up and ran toward the crowd.

Shaking her head at his fearlessness, she picked up her tepee cover and started to work.

Yawning and scratching his head, the young man

pushed his way to the front of the crowd. In the center, a rattlesnake lay coiled and ready to strike. Yet the snake looked odd, for hair grew on top of its head.

"The foolhardy boy is here," someone said

He ignored that as he concentrated on the strange rattlesnake. He walked right up and kicked the snake hard, knocking it away.

The crowd stepped back in fear.

Still coiled when it hit the ground, the rattlesnake struck but missed the young man.

He walked over and kicked the rattlesnake again. He kicked it four times in a row, but every time the snake struck too late. Finally the rattlesnake crawled away because it could not get revenge.

Not long afterward a small snake slithered out, sent by the rattlesnake. This one moved fast and bit the young man on the hip before gliding away.

The young man grew sick, and the shamans could do nothing to help him. Worried, they took him to the medicine man of the Carrizo, a tribe that lived on a small island off the coast.

The medicine man performed a sacred rite, then nodded knowingly. "You stepped before a big crowd and kicked a snake four times." He used sign language. "That rattlesnake sent a small snake to put this inside you." He pulled a snake jaw from the young man's hip. "Here it is."

Thankful for the help, the shamans took the young man back to his people. Soon he got well and fat.

He remained fearless as ever.

Deer Woman

A young woman went into the woods and saw several deer. She moved with great stealth toward them. When they bounded away, she followed. She frequently went back to stay with them. One day she did not return to camp.

Her parents grew worried. Several hunters mounted horses and set out to find her. They trailed her to an area of hills, flats, and creosote bushes.

She ran there with the deer. They called to her, but she did not reply. They circled her and the deer. Several hunters headed the deer toward the men on the other side. They let the deer pass out of the circle. The young woman ran after the deer on all fours, so they roped her. She bawled and bucked like a deer.

When the hunters got close to her, she blinked and rolled her eyes like a deer. They tried to get her to speak, but she said nothing.

They slowly led her back to camp with the rope tied so as not to choke her. They tied her to a tree outside of camp. She jerked and snorted like a deer as she tried to get away. Whenever anyone came near, she shied and snorted.

Her parents prepared food and tried to get her to eat. She ignored the food, looking everywhere but at the people.

"We must not untie her until she eats our food," one hunter said.

"Maybe she will be better in the morning," her parents said. "But we fear she will die if we keep her in our camp."

They all went to sleep in their tepees.

In the morning, she was gone.

"She is ours no more," her parents said.

After a few days the hunters followed the young woman back to the hills. Nothing had changed. Sadly, they turned their horses toward camp.

And she ran with the deer.

History

Athabascans flowed out of western Canada as they followed the expanding grasslands of the Central Plains into Texas and New Mexico. They carved out territory from the high mountain desert to the wind-swept prairies. They hunted on foot and gathered wild plants.

The Pueblos called them Apaches de Nabahu, or Enemies of the Cultivated Fields. The Apaches knew themselves to be Tende or Diné, meaning the People.

Part of the southern branch of the Athabascan language group, the Apache and Navajo migrated southward together from 1100 to 1400, but they separated about 1640 when they acquired horses. The Apache swept over the land from the Arkansas River in Kansas to Northern Mexico and from Central Texas to Central Arizona. This vast area came to be called Apachería.

Separated by the Rio Grande in the west, the Apache developed into the Western and Eastern bands. In the east the Jicarilla, the Mescaleros, the Kiowa-Apache, and the Lipan staked out their Apachería.

A nomadic people, Apaches tracked the huge buffalo herds that fed on grassland northward in the summer, then southward in the winter. They depended on buffalo for food, shelter, clothes, and implements. They traded with the Pueblos of New Mexico, exchanging buffalo products and salt for cotton blankets, pottery, and corn.

Lipan Apaches also gathered fruit, nuts, and wild plants. They learned to track and hide with enough expertise to sneak up and touch an enemy or a wild animal, which they called counting coup. They hunted small game with traps, snares, throwing sticks, bows and arrows, and spears.

They built villages of round wickiups made of bent saplings covered with leaves. They lived there when they cultivated fields of corn, beans, pumpkins, and watermelons. This tied them to the land twice a year during planting and harvesting seasons.

Lipans lived in groups of extended families, who stayed close to other groups so they could unite as a band for offense or defense. They chose a group leader who acted as chief for decisions and ceremonies. A band chief selected by all the groups led them when necessary, but they were an independent people who required little organization.

After a woman married, her husband moved into her tepee or wickiup. He worked and hunted for her family. If she died, he remained with her family, who usually found him a new wife from within the family. If he died, his family might bring a cousin or brother to her for marriage. Sometimes but not often, a man might marry two sisters or two cousins.

When on the hunt, Lipans lived in tepees of buffalo hide stretched across a frame of light poles, usually sotol stalks, tied together at the top. A smoke-hole was left at the top and an entrance hole could be covered with a hide. Large tepees might hold a dozen people, with beds made of deep piles of grass or cedar twigs covered by hides with the fur side up.

Men wore a buckskin breechclout, leggings, and moccasins, and in winter added a poncho of deerskin or buffalo robe decorated with beadwork and fringe. Women wore a three-skin dress made of a two-skin skirt and one-skin top decorated with fringe along the length of the sleeves and the hem. They might also wear beaded and fringed thigh-high boots for special ceremonies. They added a buffalo robe in winter.

Warriors cut their hair off above the ear on the left side but let it grow long then folded and tied to shoulder length on the right. They pierced their left ear six to eight times and wore earrings of copper wire and beads. They also plucked out all their facial hair and painted their face in symbolic designs when preparing for war. Women usually wore their hair in one long plait down the back, then added earrings and necklaces for decoration.

Shamans guided the Lipan spiritual life, and they conducted rituals to cure the sick, help find game, and foretell an enemy's approach. They could handle snakes, predict an eclipse of the moon, and make medicine from a wide variety of wild plants. They conducted Long Life ceremonies based on ancient myths through song and dance and costume.

The people used porcupine quills and beadwork to decorate leather pouches, moccasins, rattles, quivers, and other special pieces. They mastered the technique of tanning animal hides to make the skin strong and supple for use. Hunters and warriors depended on the ability to make fine arrowheads, knife blades, axes, and awls from flint.

Late into the nineteenth century, a Lipan hunter still preferred his bow and arrow over a single-barreled, muzzle-loading rifle. A warrior could shoot a dozen arrows while a man loaded a gun once. If warriors could draw the gunfire of their enemies at the same time, then the enemies were at Lipan mercy unless they hurriedly retreated. Warriors could present and string a bow then shoot an arrow almost as quickly as a soldier could shoot a rifle.

About four feet in length, Lipan bows were made of seasoned mulberry wood with bowstrings of twisted deer or bison sinews. Arrows whittled from hard wood had three feathers and a flint or iron point while children's arrows had two feathers. Hunters took great care of bows and arrows, for a damp bowstring had little snap and warped arrows would not fly true.

By 1500 the Lipan Apache had taken the Pueblo meat-for-corn trade away from the Wichita and forced the Caddo traders to use routes farther south to reach the Pueblos. This began an enmity that lasted many years.

Apaches first encountered the Spanish in 1541 when Francisco Vázquez de Coronado and his people journeyed to Quivera, the Wichita, in central Kansas. After 1656 Spaniards enslaved many of the Pueblos, including Apaches, and forced them to work ranches and mines and build Catholic missions. Many Apaches escaped, then fought back by raiding and stealing horses.

No power could stand against the Apache until a new force emerged from the north. At the turn of the eighteenth century, Comanches drove down into Apachería, riding horses they bred and carrying firearms they traded from the French. The Comanche learned where Apaches lived during planting and harvesting seasons, then they raided vulnerable villages. Spaniards established colonies on Lipan land, plowing under ground needed for buffalo and horse, sending out soldiers and missionaries.

Squeezed between enemies on all sides, the Navajo to the west, Spanish settlements to the west and southwest, Caddo tribes in the east, and the Comanche at the Red River, several Apache bands migrated for safety into New Mexico and Arizona. The Lipan stayed in Texas, but they continued to move south and east to survive and find peace. They adapted to new environments, even living for a time on the Gulf Coast.

During the eighteenth century, the Spanish established several missions to attract Lipans and to keep peace for their colonies. The Lipan distrusted the missions, but they lived near them at various times. In 1757 the Lipan Apache band living at San Saba Mission was estimated at 3,000 people.

The Lipan adjusted their trade route after the arrival of the Comanche to form the Attakapan-Tonkawa-Apache trade network that extended across the south of Texas. These Indians worked in peace together, but they fought and raided tribes of the Caddo-Wichita-Comanche northern trade network. This enmity continued as Lipans and Tonkawas later scouted for the United States army against Comanches and their allies.

Eventually Anglo-American diseases, Spanish hostilities, and Comanche, Kiowa, and Wichita raids greatly reduced the Lipan population. Yet Lipans continued to fight back. The men turned hunting skills into warrior skills. The women found new food sources, keeping their children and families alive.

In 1821 Spanish rule of Texas passed to the Mexican government, and the Lipan band at Laredo was estimated at 1,500 people. In 1822 Lipan leaders traveled to Mexico City to sign a peace treaty and alliance against the Comanche.

Lipans helped Anglo-Texans win independence from Mexico in 1836, then signed a treaty with the Republic of Texas in 1838 at Live Oak Point near San Antonio. In 1842 Anglo-Texans broke the treaty with attacks on Lipans, forcing them to move into Mexico near the Mescalero Apaches. In order to survive, they raided north across the border to take what once belonged to them.

When Texas became a state in 1845, the United States government officially took over control of the Indians, and the Lipans were sent to newly established forts. In 1852 the Lipan Apache band at Fort Belknap was estimated at 150 people, and in 1858 Lipans numbered 100 at Fort Clark.

In 1867 Lipan Apaches in Texas were moved as prisoners of war to Fort Griffin. At the same time a number of Lipans escaped to Laredo in Nuevo Leon, Mexico and to a second village at Cerralvo in a mountain region for better protection from Anglo-Americans. Although raided by Anglo-Texans and Mexican soldiers, the Lipan kept their people and villages alive. By 1870 they numbered only twenty-six at Fort Griffin.

The United States army sent 400 soldiers in 1873 across the Mexican border to exterminate the Lipan Apache and destroy their villages. They were successful, and most of the few Lipan survivors were sent to the Mescalero Reservation in New Mexico.

By 1885 only seventeen Lipans remained alive at Fort

Griffin, and they were moved with the Tonkawas to the old Nez Percé reservation in northern Indian Territory. In 1905 the Lipans still in Mexico rejoined their people on the Mescalero Reservation.

In 1924 Lipan Apaches, as well as other Indians, received United States citizenship.

The Lipan Apache band signed a peace treaty with the United States in San Antonio, Texas in 1976, then the official document was transferred to the Mescalero Reservation.

Today Lipan Apaches live in Texas, Oklahoma, and with the Mescalero Apache in New Mexico. They maintain their heritage and traditions in song, dance, and myth.

Wichita Confederacy

This design is based on a Spider and Fire motif found
throughout the Southeast.

---◆---

Myths and Legends

---◆---

Escape from Sun Buzzard

Geleazigits, or Thunderbird Woman, Wekskuni-widiks, or Little-Big-Belly-Boy, and Skiwis, or Libertine, lived together in a large grass lodge with an ancient cottonwood tree shading the north door.

Thunderbird Woman cooked and hauled wood. Little-Big-Belly-Boy carried all the water. And Libertine hunted, for he was a strong man with many powers. He could carry a whole buffalo home after he killed one.

One morning when Libertine left to hunt, a blade of grass fell on his back, knocking him to the ground. He could not get up, for somehow he could lift big things but not little ones. He called for Little-Big-Belly-Boy's help.

Little-Big-Belly-Boy came running, then laughed when he saw Libertine's situation. He decided to have some fun, so he left Libertine under the blade of grass until he was all worn out. When he took off the grass, Libertine went home instead of out to hunt.

Libertine was so sore that he pulled a cottonwood tree out by its roots and stood it on his back. He got Little-Big-Belly-Boy to stack more wood around the root, then set the wood on fire until it got hot. When Libertine took it all off his back he was almost healed. The next day he went out to hunt again. He stayed away until late at night, then he brought a live buffalo home with him.

Early the next morning Little-Big-Belly-Boy started to step outside, but he saw a buffalo standing at the door as mad as can be. The buffalo drove him back inside.

Libertine lay late in bed, laughing because Little-Big-Belly-Boy could not go outside.

"Move that buffalo," Little-Big-Belly-Boy said.

"I will, but I am too tired to get up right now," Libertine said.

"I want to go outside."

Libertine laughed harder.

"I need a new robe," Little-Big-Belly-Boy said. "Will you kill that buffalo and make me a robe?"

Libertine got up and stepped outside. He picked up the buffalo by the horns, shook it, and he had a robe for Little-Big-Belly-Boy.

Later Little-Big-Belly-Boy decided to get even with Libertine. He caught a mouse, tied it by the neck, and put it by the door.

When Libertine got up the next morning he started to step outside, but he saw the mouse. Frightened, he jumped back inside.

"Let that mouse go," he called.

Little-Big-Belly-Boy laughed, staying in bed.

"I need to go outside."

Finally Little-Big-Belly-Boy got up.

"Will you make me a mouse robe?"

Little-Big-Belly-Boy stepped outside, picked up the mouse, shook it, and handed Libertine a mouse robe.

When Libertine got into bed that night, he could not put on the mouse robe because it was too heavy. Little-Big-Belly-Boy put the robe on for him. Later in the night he could not turn over for the weight of the robe, so Little-Big-Belly-Boy pulled the mouse robe off him.

They all lived happily together until one day Little-Big-Belly-Boy looked sad and would not eat.

"What is the matter?" Libertine asked.

"I had a vision that a powerful force is coming to get me."

"I am powerful," Libertine said. He shot an arrow at the tree in front of the lodge and it went all the way through. "I will protect you."

"You are not strong enough. This one has more power than you."

"Do not worry. I will find some way to protect you."

Later Little-Big-Belly-Boy ran inside the lodge from playing outside. "My enemy is coming."

"Stay here. I will protect you."

Libertine picked up bow and arrows, then stepped outside. From the north it looked like a great dark cloud rushing toward them, but it was Aitskadarwiya, or Sun Buzzard. The huge bird had wings, tail, and head covered with small, sharp flint stones, and its bill looked like a sharp stone.

Sun Buzzard perched on the cottonwood tree.

Libertine raised his bow and shot four arrows straight at the bird. Not one penetrated Sun Buzzard's stone body.

Instead Sun Buzzard grew furious, flew down, plucked Libertine off the ground, and carried him north.

Sun Buzzard flew far. Libertine watched where they went, then he saw a great body of water before they came to a small island. The bird threw Libertine down into a nest in a high tree and flew on toward the east.

Several young buzzards pecked at him, but he pushed them back. He looked over the edge of the nest and saw piles of human skulls and bones littering the ground under the tree. Now he knew that Sun Buzzard frequently stole people to feed to the young.

He picked up a young buzzard. "Whose child are you?"

"I belong to Cold Weather Followed by Blizzard."

He threw that young one out of the nest and killed it.

He picked up another. "Whose child are you?"

"I belong to Nice Clear Weather."

He set that young one back in the nest and let it live.

He picked up another one. "Whose child are you?"

"I belong to Hard Rain Followed by Hard Wind."

He threw that one out of the nest and killed it.

He picked up the last one. "Whose child are you?"

"I belong to Foggy Day.

He set this young one back in the nest because everyone liked that weather.

After he killed those two of Sun Buzzard's children, he climbed out of the nest and down the tree. He had to get across the water, but he had nothing but his bow. He took off his bowstring, then he stretched it until it was long enough to reach across the water. He raised it high and swung it hard. When it hit, the water parted for him.

He ran through the dry channel to the other side before the water closed behind him. He walked long and hard, traveling as fast as he could to get home before Sun Buzzard got him again.

Finally he arrived at his lodge. Thunderbird Woman and Little-Big-Belly-Boy were glad to see him. They lived happily there for a long time, until Libertine saw Sun Buzzard coming for them. They stepped outside as the bird lit in the cottonwood tree again.

Thunderbird Woman led them toward the mountains near their lodge. When they reached the mountains, Libertine carried them on his back to keep them safe. As he went through, the rocks closed behind them.

After a time, they sat down to rest in a rock cave.

Libertine checked to see if Sun Buzzard still followed them, and he heard the great bird outside. They all listened to Sun Buzzard slowly get closer.

Finally Sun Buzzard, weakened after coming through the rock, struggled into the cave, then fell over to one side. Libertine killed Sun Buzzard.

They returned to their lodge, but they watched the mountains. Soon Sun Buzzard flew out with broken bill and chipped wings.

"I fear Sun Buzzard will come for me again," Libertine said. "I will go into the woods, and from now on you may find me on dead wood."

"We will all change," Thunderbird Woman said.

Libertine became Big-Red-Water-Worm. Thunderbird Woman went toward the north, calling herself Rain Woman. Little-Big-Belly-Boy flew to the prairie as Dry-Grass-Bird.

Sun Buzzard returned to dwell in the heat at the darkness in the back of the Sun.

Swift Hawks and the Buffalo Women

A young man lived with his father, mother, and sister near a village. He kept four ferocious dogs at home. No one could ever visit even though he kept his dogs tied up.

Wesakakuts, or White Wolf, was the name of the white dog. Watayar, or Fox, was the name of the black dog. Woks, or Panther, was the name of the red dog.

Wedadadiyakista, or Bear, was the name of the copper dog.

He liked to hunt, and he killed all types of game such as deer, buffalo, and turkey. When he brought game home, the family dressed it, then ate and used it for clothes.

One day before he left to hunt, he turned to his family. "If my dogs act uneasy while I am gone, set them loose because it will mean I am in trouble."

"I will watch them," his sister said.

He turned north in search of game. He walked briskly for some time before he met two women who wore buffalo robes. Their faces were tattooed in the pattern of his people, so he stopped to talk.

"What do you hunt?" one asked.

"Everything," he said. "Deer, turkey, buffalo."

"That is what we thought," the other woman said.

"We came to see you."

"Will you walk with us?"

He nodded in agreement, then set out north again. They walked with him.

"How would you escape if an enemy attacked you?" one woman asked.

"I could command myself to turn into a small ant."

The women walked faster, and he kept up with them.

"Surely you can do more than that to escape," the other woman said.

"I could command myself to turn into a small bird and hide in the grass."

They continued walking toward the north, faster and faster.

"Do you have any other means to escape an enemy?"

"I have a bow and four arrows, two painted black and

two painted red. I could shoot them, and they would carry me far."

"Can you run fast?"

"I can run fast, even faster from danger."

"Can you do anything else to stay out of danger?"

"No. That is all."

They continued to walk and soon went over a hill. On the other side grazed a large herd of buffalo. He knew he looked at danger, but he walked with the women close to the herd. The women turned into buffalo.

He spoke a command, became an ant, and disappeared into the tall grass.

"How can that hunter get out of danger?" the buffalo asked.

"Stamp the ground all over the place where he disappeared," the buffalo women said.

The buffalo stamped and stamped with their sharp hooves.

Some distance from the herd, the young man leaped to his feet and ran away.

The buffalo saw him and gave chase, thundering across the prairie.

When the herd was almost upon him, he commanded himself to turn into a small bird. He ran swiftly across the prairie.

"What must we do now?" the buffalo asked.

"You must tramp all over the ground," the buffalo women said.

Ahead of the buffalo, the young man got to his feet and ran hard for his life.

The buffalo saw him and gave chase again. When they were almost upon him, he notched one of his arrows. He shot the black arrow first, and it carried him through the air. When he came down, he ran again. Soon the buffalo were almost upon him. He shot another arrow, and it carried him a long way. He came down and ran again, but the buffalo caught up with him. He shot another arrow, ran, then another. When he had nothing else to use, he climbed an elm tree and clung to it. The buffalo gathered around and hooked the trunk with their horns.

At his home, the dogs grew so restless that his father cut the ropes from their necks. They raced toward the north, the white in the lead, followed by the black, the red, the copper. They trailed until they reached the elm tree. The buffalo were about to knock it down. Barking and biting, they ran off the buffalo herd, chasing them into the distance.

He climbed down from the tree and walked home, knowing he would never see his dogs again. After his family learned what happened, they decided they could no longer safely live in that place.

As they left, their home became a tree, their dressed meat changed into the bark, and they flew away as Swift Hawks.

Spider Woman and Spider Man

Once two villages stood side by side with only a wide trail that ran north and south to separate them. Two chiefs led their people in harmony. They grew crops, hunted game, and sent out war parties.

The chief who lived in the village on the west side of

the trail raised a respected daughter. The chief who lived in the village on the east side of the trail raised a brave son. Both chiefs grew frustrated when their beloved children found no one within their own village to marry.

As it happened the son and daughter of the two chiefs liked to sleep outside their parents' lodges in the summer. Special sleeping places were constructed of four tall forked poles placed vertically in the ground, then crossed by two long poles laid horizontally in the forks. Braided willow mats made a floor covered with soft buffalo hides sewn together. A tall ladder was used to reach the beds, then the ladder was taken down each night so no one could get up there.

One dark night with only a sliver of moon in the sky the ladders were forgotten and left in place. The chief's son lay awake, thinking about the chief's daughter in the village across the trail. The chief's daughter thought about the chief's son, so close and yet so far away. Both got up and climbed down their ladders.

In the middle of the trail between the villages, they saw the dark shadow of another person. They stopped.

"Where are you going?" The chief's son tried to recognize the woman, but the night was dark.

"I plan to see the chief's son." The chief's daughter thought she recognized the young man's voice. "Where are you going?"

"I plan to see the chief's daughter." The young woman's voice sounded familiar to him.

"I am the chief's daughter."

"I am the chief's son."

They laughed, finally recognizing each other.

"I understand you refused many young warriors," the chief's son said.

"Yes, I have. But I hear you find no one you want to marry in your village."

"That is true." He took her hand. "I would like to marry you."

She squeezed his hand. "I came to marry you."

He smiled. "As chiefs, both our fathers will want us to live with them."

"Yes. Still it is right for a husband to live with his wife in her mother's lodge."

"I know. But will you come to live at my mother's lodge?" he asked.

She smiled. "Perhaps we will live for a while with your family, then with mine. That way both chiefs will be happy."

They walked hand in hand into the east village, then climbed the ladder to his bed. That night they happily married each other.

Early the next morning when the chief's son did not come down to take an early morning bath in the stream as usual, the chief grew concerned.

Soon it was discovered that his son had taken a wife in the night. Everyone in the family rejoiced that she was the chief's daughter of the west village. While the newly married couple ate food in the chief's lodge, a message was sent to the other chief.

In the meantime the chief of the west village sent out people to find his daughter. Ketox, or Coyote, looked in the east village for the chief's daughter, for he always had the chief's best interests at heart. He found her, then returned with his report.

The west village chief was glad to learn his daughter had married the chief of the east village's son. Still he planned for her to bring her new husband to live with her family as was only proper.

A few years later, a son was born to the couple who now lived in her mother's west village lodge. Everyone in both villages rejoiced. As was the custom, women came for the child and carried him around to their lodges so all could see and share the joy of a newborn. When the baby needed to nurse, a woman would bring him back to his mother. If the child was kept too long, Coyote would walk around both villages and find out who had the boy. Soon the child would be back in his mother's arms.

Early one morning when everyone in the villages was still in bed, an elder came to the chief's daughter.

"Let me take the baby now," Old Woman said.

"It is early."

"Yes. With so many wanting to hold your son, I cannot be sure of getting him during the day."

"He will be hungry soon, so do not keep him long." Still in bed, the chief's daughter reached for her baby, took him out of his cradle board, and handed him to the older woman.

"I will do well by him." She accepted the baby, then walked out of the lodge, leaning on her walking stick.

After a time the chief's daughter needed to nurse her son. She waited. When the elder did not bring him back, she sent Coyote to look for him in the villages. Word went round, but no woman brought the baby back. Soon everyone grew alarmed.

The chiefs ordered their warriors to search their villages, but they could not find the child either. Next they called on all those with great powers to find their grandchild. When these people arrived at the chiefs' lodges, they were promised that the one who found the child would become a chief in the villages. This promise included all beings with power, including four-leggeds and winged-ones. Time passed but not a single one found the trail of the woman who had taken the child.

One day Spider Woman, a woman of power, came to the lodge.

"If you agree, I will look for your stolen child."

"Please try," the chief's daughter said. "I miss him so and I worry night and day."

"I will do exactly what the one who stole your son did and see if I can pick up her trail."

Spider Woman left the lodge, then returned early the next morning when everyone in the villages was still asleep. She walked with a walking stick, repeated the same words, reached toward the mother's empty hands, then turned and stepped out of the lodge. When her feet touched the ground, she picked up the trail of Old Woman, a powerful being.

She knew Old Woman had gone underground with the baby. She followed the trail into the earth and then tracked the child underground all day long. Finally she lost the trail and could not pick it up again. She returned to the villages in defeat, then she sought out the chiefs and the parents of the child.

"Old Woman took your child. She has greater power than I do," Spider Woman said. "I do not know how you will ever find him again. Yet do not give up hope."

Tears filled the chief's daughter's eyes, and she looked to her husband for support.

The chiefs turned to their people and announced a big hunting trip because they wanted to be far away from the sad memories. A few days later the people packed up and started on the trail.

Coyote came to the chief of the west village. "I am

taking my family to the timber. We will live there until you return. I do not wish to be far from the villages in case the boy should somehow return."

"Thank you." The chief shook his head. "But I fear we will never see my grandson again."

While the people left on the hunt, Coyote led his large family to a creek in the woods where they could hunt, fish, and gather nuts and berries. They would also watch over the villages, because Coyote hoped to recover the child and be named a chief.

One day Coyote stood on the bank of the creek and tried to shoot fish under the water with arrows. Luck was on the side of the fish and his frustration grew.

"Go ahead, shoot a fish."

Coyote yelped in surprise at the unexpected voice and almost fell in the creek. He whirled around to see a man standing behind him.

"You scared me! I thought my family was the only one living around here."

"I am Spider Man. I live near here."

Coyote knew Spider Man's other name was Kiatsatoria, or Moving Fire. He was known in the villages as the most powerful man of all. If anyone called, "Spider Man has come," they all raced into their lodges.

He had never seen any man dressed like Spider Man, and he greatly admired his clothes. Spider Man wore a feather on his head, a robe with an arrow for a closure on his chest, and he had four other arrows.

"Where do you live?" Coyote asked.

"Nearby. When I go hunting I pass your place. Today I decided to stop and see you."

"I am glad you did." Coyote looked over Spider Man again. "I admire your clothes. I would like to dress like you, if you do not mind."

"Not at all."

Spider Man grabbed Coyote and threw him in the stream. Coyote splashed to the surface, sputtering in fury.

"Look at yourself in the water."

Coyote glanced down, then laughed in surprise. He appeared exactly as Spider Man.

"Are you hungry?" Spider Man asked.

"I am always hungry."

"Come to my place and eat. It is not far from your lodge."

They walked to Spider Man's lodge, then sat down inside by the center fire. A piece of meat on a stick roasted over the fire.

"Try this." Spider Man handed Coyote the meat. "You will like it."

"Thank you."

Coyote ate the tasty meat until there was only a small bit left on the stick. Spider took it from him, turned the stick, and the meat was large again. He handed it back. Coyote looked at the meat in surprise, then he continued eating and turning the stick until he was full.

"Are you brave?" Spider Man asked.

"Yes, I am."

"Good. I want you to go after the chiefs' grandson."

"You know where he is? We looked everywhere."

"I know. You must hurry. The boy is almost scorched to death."

Coyote stood up. "I am ready right now."

"Wait. I will give you power to go into the place where the child is kept, but you must follow several rules to safely complete your task."

"Tell me."

Later Coyote went home to his family. He gave the meat to them and showed them how to use it. He told his wife that from now on they would live as sister and brother rather than wife and husband, and they would sleep in separate beds. When all was in order at his lodge, he went back to Spider Man.

"You have done all I asked?" Spider Man watched Coyote.

"Yes. I am ready."

"You must be very brave. You will encounter four dangerous beings on your journey, but do not let them scare you. Remember, the child will die without your help."

"I am ready."

"Then go."

Coyote carried his bow and Spider Man's four arrows in his quiver when he set out on his journey. He traveled far and fast over trails known and unknown. Nothing stopped him until he came to the first guardian of Old Woman's land.

Chearppeschaux, or Headless Man, chased Coyote back down the trail. "You cannot pass."

"I am Spider Man. You may not stop me. I have power." Coyote ran around Headless Man until the powerful being faced north.

"Why do you come here?" Headless Man asked. "This is Old Woman's land, not yours."

"I seek the child."

"You are determined to go after the boy no matter the difficulty to you."

"Yes, I am."

"Go then. I cannot stop you. You travel the right trail now. But remember, you must be brave to rescue the child."

"I am brave."

Coyote stuck his feet tight to the ground, then continued on his journey. Soon he came to the next powerful being.

Second Headless Man chased Coyote back down the trail. "You may not pass."

"I am Spider Man. You may not stop me. I have great power." Coyote ran around Headless Man until the being faced north.

"Only a fool would seek the child in Old Woman's land. Turn back."

"I am no fool," Coyote said. "And I will pass."

"Spider Man," Headless Man said. "I see you are determined to recover the boy. He was carried by here, but if you rescue him you must be clever."

"I am clever."

Coyote stuck his feet tight to the ground, then continued on his journey. Soon he came to Third Headless Man who brandished his war club. Coyote ran around this powerful being until he faced north.

"I am Spider Man. You may not stop me. I have great power."

"Spider Man, it is true you have great power, but if you are not crafty, you will never rescue the child."

"I am crafty."

Coyote stuck his feet tight to the ground, then continued on his journey. After a time he reached Fourth Headless Man who stood in his way. Coyote ran around the powerful being until he faced north.

"Spider Man, you passed the other three guardians. Your power has grown in Old Woman's land," Headless Man said. "You are determined to rescue the child. I cannot stop you, but know that no other being has gotten through to here. Still, you must be strong to win."

"I am strong."

Coyote stuck his feet tight to the ground, then continued on his journey.

Finally he reached a village. As he moved toward the west side, he watched flames leap from the huge central fire. The chiefs' grandchild hung from a pole where he was scorched every night.

When Coyote was in position, he notched an arrow and sent it flying toward the east where it stuck the ground and started a fire. He sent the next arrow south to start a fire. One flew west to start a fire. And he shot an arrow north to start a fire.

With the village ringed with fire, the people ran here and there in fear and panic. He rushed past them to rescue the chiefs' grandchild.

"Spider Man comes!" he shouted, knowing how it would affect them.

The people guarding the baby saw him, heard him, and ran harder, repeating his words. Soon everyone in the village cried, "Spider Man comes for the child," as they tried to escape him and the raging fires.

Coyote gently lifted the baby down from the pole and looked about at the chaos. If he did not hurry, he and the child would both burn alive. He ran hard, barely ahead of the flames. The fire cut off his escape, so he twisted and turned, making progress then losing ground until he finally ran out of the burning village.

He heard an explosion .behind him, then thunder shook the earth and lightning struck at him as he raced across open ground. Rocks and stone flew around him, striking his robe, battering his head. Old Woman was a powerful being, but he carried the power of Spider Man.

As the others burned, he escaped.

He sank down to the ground and bowed his head in exhaustion. The child cried, but he rocked the boy until he was comforted and fell asleep.

Soon Coyote started home. When he reached Fourth Headless Man, he made the creature carry the child on his back until he sank to his knees in exhaustion.

"Please release me without harm," Headless Man said.

"In the name of Spider Man, I cannot do that."

Spider Man had warned Coyote not to listen to their pleas, and he did not. He struck Headless Man on the head with his bow and killed him. He continued his journey, following the same pattern with each Headless Man until he killed the last one.

After traveling a great distance, he finally reached home, and Spider Man.

"I saved the chiefs' grandchild." Coyote handed the boy to Spider Man, thinking that now he would be made a chief in the villages.

Spider Man carried the suffering child to the stream, then dropped him in the water. The boy sank beneath the surface.

"Rise, grandchild of great chiefs," Spider Man said.

The boy rose and floated on top of the water.

Spider Man lifted the healed boy from the stream, then turned to Coyote. "Bring me one of your children who is the same age as this one.

Coyote hurried home, greeted his wife as his sister, explained his mission, then brought his own child back to Spider Man.

Spider Man threw Coyote's boy in the water where he sank deep.

"Rise, boy who will be grandchild of great chiefs."

Coyote's child floated to the surface, and Spider Man lifted him from the stream. Now the boy looked exactly like the chiefs' grandchild.

They carried the identical boys back to Spider Man's lodge, a place that no one else could see.

Coyote received this same power to hide his home, but Spider Man also warned him that he must live apart from women because Spider Man was a single man. If Coyote did this, he would retain all the powers of Spider Man.

After the people of the two villages returned from their hunting trip, Spider Man sent Coyote to them.

Coyote walked into the villages, but no one recognized him. A man led him to a central large grass lodge, then indicated that he should enter. Inside sat both chiefs with many counselors. They all saw Coyote as a powerful stranger, a man of fine clothes and important demeanor.

"You are welcome," the east village chief said.

"But you will find us poor company," the west village chief said.

"Our grandchild was stolen."

"We went on a hunt to ease our pain and are just back."

"Did it help?" Coyote asked.

"No," both chiefs agreed.

"Then hurt no longer." Coyote sat down across the fire from them. "I am the man you once called Coyote. I remained behind to watch the villages, and now I have a tale for you."

When Coyote completed his story, everyone wept in happiness.

"Hurry!" the chiefs commanded. "Go and bring back our beloved grandchild."

"You will find my lodge at the edge of the woods near the fork of the stream," Coyote said.

Several of the chiefs' warriors set out, and Coyote followed. When the men could not find Coyote's place, they turned in confusion to him.

Coyote revealed his power by taking them to see what they could not see before. They were amazed and impressed. They placed the two boys on a large robe and carried them back to the villages.

When they arrived at the villages, the boy's parents and grandparents rushed out to see him. They stopped in confusion at the sight of the identical children.

"Which one is your son?" Coyote asked.

They could not tell, so Coyote pointed out the chiefs' son. The daughter of the chief picked up one boy, and the son of the chief picked up the other child.

"You did well, Coyote," the chiefs said. "A new home will be built for you and a separate one for your former wife and family. Now you have the power of a great chief."

"Please let us adopt your son to be raised with our own," the west village chief's daughter said.

"You may do that," Coyote agreed as he looked around at the people of the villages. He had exactly what he always wanted. He could not ask for more.

Coyote lived in the villages for a long time. He saw his former wife and children, taught his now adopted son to shoot arrows, and helped other people. He called on Spider Man as he had been told to do.

No matter how many women came to him at night for marriage, he turned them all down. He did not forget

Spider Man's warning because he wanted to keep his power.

Yet time passed and he grew accustomed to being a powerful chief, and the fact that he had once been Coyote faded in his mind. He called on Spider Man less.

After a while he took a notion that there might be a woman for him, but only one. Nekastarahars, or Woman-Who-Wears-Shell-Rattles, was a beautiful, powerful woman. He decided if she ever came to his lodge, he would accept her for a wife. Yet he did not expect her to come to him.

One night he heard shells rattling as Woman-Who-Wears-Shell-Rattles neared his lodge. He watched her as she entered his home, then he accepted her into his bed as his wife.

Immediately Spider Man knew that the pact had been broken, and he took away Coyote's great power.

In the morning Woman-Who-Wears-Shell-Rattles awoke to see a true coyote lying beside her in the bed. She screamed in fear. Coyote awakened, then raced from the lodge in fright. He did not stop running until he reached the wilderness where he remains today.

When the chiefs learned what happened, they called the people together.

"Someone wronged us," the east village chief said.

"Another might wrong us too," the west village chief said.

"You should go wherever you want to go."

"You may want to become animals."

"Do as you wish."

Some of the people left the villages, in twos or families or groups. A few turned into four-leggeds, others winged-ones. Many stayed. The chiefs and their families, even Coyote's adopted son, remained in the villages as people.

Not-Know-Who-You-Are Saves the People

Not-Know-Who-You-Are lived in a large village that sent out war parties all the time. When warriors returned they brought home scalps and captives. At night the people celebrated with victory dances and scalp dances.

One time during a celebration, Not-Know-Who-You-Are heard crying instead of dancing. He wondered why.

After he returned from the next long war party, he celebrated with his village at a scalp dance. Late in the night he heard crying instead of dancing. Again he wondered why.

He asked around and learned that somebody had been stolen from the dance by a wild animal. He did not like this at all. He decided to send out a war party. When they returned home, he would kill the animal when it came to the dance.

Not-Know-Who-You-Are organized a war party the next day and went on the warpath. They killed many people and took many scalps. When they returned, the people danced late into the night. Not-Know-Who-You-Are watched for the animal to appear, but he saw nothing unusual. Finally he heard people crying, and he discovered that somebody had been carried away again.

Not-Know-Who-You-Are realized the animal had tricked him as well as other leaders. He decided he would do better some place else. He was not married, so he moved his parents and sister to another village.

Soon he organized a war party and went on the warpath. They hunted a long time. When they returned he brought scalps to show who he was to these people. Everyone celebrated at the dances. He kept watch, but still somebody screamed. He learned another person had been stolen by the animal.

Not-Know-Who-You-Are made a decision to hunt down the beast who refused to leave his people alone. It would be a dangerous mission, so he needed a good plan.

He decided on a course of action, then he cut two long poles. He peeled the bark, then marked them at the top with a burned stick. He stuck them in the ground in front of his lodge. Next he sent a crier around the village to announce that he was holding a guessing contest. Any woman who correctly guessed what the poles were for and why he had come to the village could, if she so desired, become his wife.

Many young women in the village wanted to marry him because he was a handsome, successful hunter and warrior. Soon women gathered around his lodge. Some of the women simply wanted to play the game, and they laughed and joked as they guessed amongst themselves.

A family named Nikitetswakasa, or Horned Owls, lived on the south side of the village. The parents had four daughters who decided to join the contest.

"You stay home," the older three daughters said. "You will not be able to make a correct guess."

"But I want to join the game," the youngest said.

"You are too ugly. You could never guess right."

"I may not be as beautiful as all of you, but I can guess."

"Even if you guessed right, that fine warrior would never marry you."

The youngest hung her head. "I will stay at home."

After the three sisters left, their father turned to the youngest one.

"Do you still want to try the guessing game?"

"Yes. But I do not want to look a fool."

"You will not. If you say exactly what I tell you to say, you will win the warrior."

"I will do exactly as you say."

With her father's words filling her head, the young woman hurried to Not-Know-Who-You-Are's lodge. People thronged around it, laughing and joking. Several women had already failed. When she saw her sisters standing in line in the crowd, she walked up to them.

"What are you doing here?" they asked.

"I am here to guess."

"Go home. You will make a fool of yourself."

"No more so than you."

"You can never guess what the poles mean."

"I will try."

She pushed past them to stand in line in the crowd. She listened to several women fail, then each of her sisters guessed. They were all wrong.

When her turn came, she walked up to the lodge. She knew the warrior lay on his bed inside as he listened to the women guess.

"Not-Know-Who-You-Are." She quoted her father. "You have come here and placed your poles before the women of this village. You ask them to guess the meaning of these poles, and the one who does so will become your wife. I am that one. I will make a correct guess.

"First, the marks on these poles do not affect the poles

in any way. Second, at your old village the people went on war parties and returned with scalps and captives. While they danced and sang at night in celebration, they were interrupted by crying because an animal stole somebody away.

"Third, you decided to stop this beast by going on the warpath yourself and bringing back scalps and captives. At the dances you planned to catch the animal. Instead, you lost more people.

"Fourth, you made a new plan. You decided to learn more about the beast by moving to this village. Once here you went out on a war party, then returned for more scalp and victory dances. Yet during the dancing another person was lost to the animal.

"Fifth, you made new plans. Now you are determined to follow the tracks of the beast. For that you cut two poles and marked them with a burnt stick. You plan to make the beast guess what the poles and black marks mean. When the animal fails, you will kill it, cut off the paws, and tie them to the ends of the poles.

"That is my guess."

Not-Know-Who-You-Are called from inside the lodge. "Let this woman stay. She is right. Everyone else may return to their lodges."

As the crowd dispersed, the three sisters stopped by their younger one.

"You should go home before he sees you," they said.

"I won. He will marry me."

"He will never marry someone as ugly as you. Many beautiful women guessed wrong, but surely he will still want them."

"He is an honorable warrior. He will marry me."

"You are a fool," they said. "An ugly fool."

The three sisters walked away, discussing the possibility of marrying Not-Know-Who-You-Are once the contest was forgotten.

The youngest patiently waited outside the lodge, then Not-Know-Who-You-Are's sister took her inside.

"You guessed well. I want to marry you," he said.

"I like a riddle. And a strong warrior."

After darkness, they walked to a nearby creek.

"Jump in there," he said. "Cover yourself completely with water."

"If this is another game, I am ready."

She jumped into the creek and bathed her entire body with water. When she stepped out, moonlight revealed that her physical appearance was the same, but she had been cleansed of all the hurtful remarks. Now she stood proud, a powerful young woman.

They clasped hands and walked home together.

With a powerful woman at his side, Not-Know-Who-You-Are could now go after the animal. He prepared his war bundle, then turned to his wife.

"Watch for me in the west. When I return I will hold up the sticks. If they have animal paws on them, you will know I killed the beast."

"We will dance your victory when you return."

Soon he set out, carrying the two poles. He found the animal's trail, but the tracks were old. He followed them, staying low so the beast would not see him first.

He tracked for several days before he found a fresh trail. Across bare ground and in tall grass, he saw where the animal's tail had burned everything in its wake. He followed, getting closer all the time.

Finally he dropped to the ground and crawled up to the top of a hill. He saw the beast. With surprise on his side, he stood up.

"I am Not-Know-Who-You-Are." He held up the two poles. "Can you guess what these are for?"

Caught off guard, the enraged beast raced over to him. "Those poles mean nothing to me, but I know why you are here. You want to kill me. And this is your way.

"When you lived in your former village, war parties brought back scalps and captives. At their victory dances at night, you heard crying and you wanted to know why. After you learned, you decided to go on the warpath and then catch me at your victory dance. I stole another person. You failed.

"You decided you would catch me better if you moved to another village. Again you went on the warpath and brought back scalps and captives. Again you failed."

"I am correct," the beast said. "Now I will kill you."

"Wait!" Not-Know-Who-You-Are gripped the poles. "You failed to guess correctly about the poles."

The beast appeared surprised.

"You must guess about the poles, then you may kill me if you are correct. If you are wrong, then I will kill you. It is only fair."

"The poles have nothing to do with killing me," the beast said. "Now you may require nothing more of me since I have answered all your questions."

"Let me tell you about the poles."

"That and nothing more."

"When I kill you, I will cut off your front paws and attach each one to the end of a pole, then carry them back to my people in triumph."

"I did not think of that," the beast said.

"You failed to answer all."

Not-Know-Who-You-Are unstrung his bow, then used

the string to kill the beast. He cut off the front paws and attached them to the poles. Woxis, or Spike Tail Mountain Lion, would hurt his people no more.

After traveling for many days, Not-Know-Who-You-Are arrived at the hill near his village. He held up the poles with Mountain Lion's paws. The people saw and knew he had succeeded.

He walked to his lodge where he was welcomed by his wife. He stuck the poles in the ground in front of his home, then the village celebrated with dances that lasted night after night.

War parties went out and returned victorious. They brought back scalps and captives, then danced at night. Mountain Lion hurt them no more. Not-Know-Who-You-Are's wife remained proud of him throughout their lives.

Turtle's War Party

In a village where Turtle lived, the chief made it known that his daughter would marry the warrior who brought the chief a red-haired scalp. This was a difficult task and would prove to the chief if the warrior deserved his beloved daughter.

White Geese spied for the Wasps, a red-haired people, so no one could sneak up on them. Whenever anyone tried to reach the Wasps, the White Geese warned them. Many warriors failed in their attempt to get a red-haired scalp.

Turtle knew all this only too well, so one day he turned to his mother. "Will you make me a pair of moccasins and prepare cornmeal to take with me?"

"Where are you going, my son?"

"I want to get a red-haired scalp."

"No. It is not safe. Those who try always die."

"I believe I can do it, and I intend to try."

She bowed her head in agreement, knowing she could not stop her son, then did as he asked.

Soon Turtle started out with new moccasins and plenty of cornmeal. He walked west where the Wasps were known to live. After a time he saw a hill with smoke coming out of its top. Curious, he decided to see who lived there.

Mole, Ishuhukehhas, welcomed him inside.

"Sit on my south side," Mole said.

Turtle sat there.

"I drew you here to go after the Wasps," Mole said. "I will help you get a red-haired scalp so you may marry the chief's daughter."

"I can use help, so it is a good plan," Turtle said.

"You may stay here while I find the Wasps."

"Thank you," Turtle said.

Mole traveled underground so as not to be seen by the White Geese and arrived at the village of the Wasps. After locating all the red-haired people, Mole hurried back to tell Turtle the good news.

Mole turned back underground, and Turtle followed until they reached the camps of the Wasps. By now night had fallen, so they waited until all had gone to sleep. Mole checked here and there to find the red-haired chief, then he came back and told Turtle were to go.

Turtle crept to the red-haired chief's lodge, cut off his

head, then rejoined Mole. They went underground and traveled hard all night long. Early the next morning they arrived at Mole's home. They rested and then Turtle started home the next day with his red-haired scalp.

When he reached his own village, he went straight to the chief's lodge. He held out the red-haired scalp.

"This scalp is for you. I did what no other warrior could do."

"I am pleased." The chief took the scalp. "Now you may live with me and marry my daughter."

"And I am proud of you," the chief's daughter said. "You will make a fine husband."

Happy with his success, Turtle hurried home to tell his mother. Grateful to have him safely back, she quickly spread the news of her son's prowess throughout the village. Soon many warriors came to hear how Turtle had triumphed where all others failed.

And Turtle told them about Mole.

Bad Boy and Warrior Women

One time in a village a chief had two sons. The older was called Bad Boy. As a powerful warrior, the chief wanted to instruct his eldest son in the use of his power, but Bad Boy would not listen. The younger son was not yet old enough to learn.

Frequently the chief went on the warpath followed by many warriors who trusted him to lead them in war. When he returned home, he always tried to persuade Bad

Boy to stay at home so he could receive his powers.

Bad Boy preferred the independence outside his father's lodge. He scrounged around the village, picking up parched corn in ash heaps to eat. He slept wherever he liked as long as it was away from others. He refused to stay in his father's lodge, and when he saw his younger brother he teased the boy to make him cry.

After a time the chief decided to change Bad Boy's bad ways. He sent out criers to bring the people to his lodge. When they arrived, he made an announcement.

"If any of you see Bad Boy among your lodges, kill or whip him. He will do no more mischief here."

They muttered about the harsh judgement, then hurried back to their lodges. A crier went to the outskirts of the village, announcing the chief's message about Bad Boy.

That evening Bad Boy heard the news, and he knew his father would surely see him dead. Late in the night he returned to his father's lodge and crawled into his own bed. Early the next morning, his family saw him.

"Father, I ask for your instructions in how to use the war bundle that you offered me."

"Are you sure?" the chief asked.

"It is time."

The chief took down the war bundle. "This is called Narwitstanaseh. Everything you need is in it. Shield, quiver, bow and arrows, tobacco pouch, and war club." He spread War-Secrets-Bundle out before his son.

"In this shield is a stuffed hawk and in each foot is a scalp. The tobacco pouch is made of dyed skunk hide with black-stone pipe and a white feather inside."

Bad Boy listened closely.

"If you set out on the warpath or attack an enemy in

their village, use the scalp in the left foot of the stuffed hawk. If you want to attack them in the wilderness, use the scalp in the right foot of the hawk."

Bad Boy nodded.

"If you decide to go on the warpath, you must ask a man to go with you as Second Leading Warrior. He will select another Second Leading Warrior. You must follow the instructions I will give you."

Bad Boy listened to what his father had to say and kept it all to himself.

On a foggy day, a day a man of great powers would choose to go on the warpath, Bad Boy decided to go. He bathed in the creek, painted his body, filled his pipe with tobacco, then went to find a Second Leading Warrior.

He arrived at a certain man's lodge. "Are you at home?" he called.

"Enter."

He stepped inside. "Please rise."

The man stood up.

Bad Boy spread his robe on the ground. "Please sit upon my robe."

The man sat on it.

Bad Boy offered his pipe.

The man took it.

"Please smoke." Bad Boy lit the pipe.

The man smoked.

"I want you to serve under me on the warpath," Bad Boy said.

"When do you want to start?"

"In a few days."

Bad Boy went home to his father's lodge. He was quiet all day and then that night he decided he should be somewhere else and show his powers.

Early the next evening he left home without telling his parents or his Second Leading Warrior. He kept going all night and all day until late the next evening. He saw a village, then a cave. He left his war bundle in the cave and walked down to the village where young people played the game of shinny.

"Bad Boy!" the boys called. "What are you doing here?"

Bad Boy waved at them, then he entered the first lodge he came across. Two elders, a man and a woman, and a young boy sat inside.

"May I stay with you?" he asked.

"We can use a young man like you to help us," the elders said.

When Bad Boy stepped outside, others called for him to live with them, but he stayed with the first lodge.

Soon he did as he had done in his father's village. He scrounged around for parched corn that had been thrown away. Sometimes others asked him to eat with them, and he always saved some for the family where he stayed. Everyone knew him as a chief's son and a bad boy, so the boys in the village played jokes on him.

When it came time, the people moved from the village for a big hunt. They traveled on foot and carried their belongings. Bad Boy followed them a long way before he remembered his war bundle in the cave. He debated about returning for it, then decided he had better go back and get it.

He walked to the cave, picked up his war bundle, and set off after the people. He hurried until he caught up with them, then he turned south and met a group of young women.

"Bad Boy," they called, "what do you have there?"

"Where did you get that war bundle?"

As they teased him, he raised his war club as if to scare them. He followed the young women.

They laughed and teased him more.

He pretended to be angry. "If you make fun of me any more, I will have to club you."

They laughed even harder as he drove them, brandishing his war club. Soon they left the hunting party behind.

"Let us set out on the warpath," Bad Boy said.

"Yes, let us do that," the young women agreed.

They made camp, then he shot a deer. They ate deer meat for supper, and the women tanned the hide so he could make a quiver. He finished it that night. He did not want the women to know how little he knew about going on the warpath, so he selected two women as his Second Leading Warriors. He instructed them as his father had taught him.

They started out the next day and traveled for fourteen days. Every evening Bad Boy killed deer and made quivers from the hides. He also made bows and arrows to ready the women for war. Every time they camped the Second Leading Warriors performed the tobacco rite with him.

"Today I go out to spy," Bad Boy said. "When I return, if I am running, I have seen an enemy. You sit down in a circle, but leave an open place for me to enter."

Bad Boy ran far and fast. He came to a small hill, then slowed down when he saw someone coming toward him. He turned around and ran back to his warriors.

When he reached them, he gave a loud whoop. "I have seen the enemy!"

He entered their circle and sat down between his two Second Leading Warriors. He knew it was a rule for a man to tell everything he saw after such a mission.

"Ask me how I traveled and found the enemy," he whispered to the one on his right.

"Ask me if I had luck while out spying and to tell the full story of my spying," he whispered to the one on his left.

They did exactly as he asked, and soon he told his warriors about his journey and his spying.

"Ask me what I thought of it all," he whispered to them both.

They asked him that too.

"I believe we should go after the enemy I saw," Bad Boy said.

All the women warriors whooped.

They set off at a fast pace, brandishing their war weapons, but soon they grew cautious so their enemy would not see them. They found the enemy walking down a creek, and they waited for him under an overhanging rock.

Bad Boy ran out to meet the enemy, the warrior women right behind. They caught Trickster by surprise, but the enemy stood and fought, for it is always better to fight than to run. Trickster shot arrow after arrow until Bad Boy finally got close enough to club him. Trickster fell dead, and Bad Boy took his scalp.

They turned back and hurried away so other enemies would not catch them. Soon they arrived home, stopping at Place-Where-Returning-Victorious-War-Party-Halted, or Nasaquatowene. Here a signal for victorious war parties was given to the village by turning back twice. The people who had returned from the hunt were surprised, so they sent out men to find who came back victorious.

Bad Boy and the warrior women were praised as they

came into the village. That night the people danced in honor of them. Afterward everyone in the village admired Bad Boy. Now he was a good boy, no longer a bad boy. The people who shared their lodge with him received compliments, food, and other provisions.

Bad Boy led many more war parties over the years, and he became a valued chief. He stayed in the village all his life, but he never married. Finally, when he was an elder, he called the people together.

"You have always known me as Bad Boy. Now is the time for me to leave you. One day I will grant a worthy young person great powers."

Bad Boy lifted his arms and rose into the sky. He flew away as a Hawk.

Coyote and Skunk Plan a Feast

One day Ketox, or Coyote, hunted game for his family. He hoped for the best, but sometimes he found nothing to eat. He was about to give up when he came across the tracks of Niwechia, or Skunk. He followed the trail, then surprised the small animal. As he started to kill Skunk, he stopped.

"You are my enemy, so I must kill you. My wife and children are hungry."

"Wait!" Skunk said. "If you let me live, I will give you the power to kill animals with more flesh than me."

"Where would I find such animals?"

"Gidisgardahits are having a medicine dance near

here. Beavers make fine food."

"But that does not help me."

"I have a plan." Skunk sidled away. "If we send for these medicine makers one at a time, we can kill many for you."

"That is a good idea."

"If you do as I tell you, you will have plenty to eat."

Soon Coyote loped away and found Beavers busy at their medicine dance.

"What do you want?" Beavers asked.

"My partner is sick and he wishes one of you to come doctor him."

"We are all medicine makers," Beavers said. "Choose one of us to go."

Coyote picked out a fat one, and the medicine maker followed him back to Skunk.

The black and white animal lay on the ground groaning and moaning.

"Where do you hurt?" Beaver asked, bending over Skunk to get a better look.

Coyote hit the medicine maker over the head, and Beaver fell over dead.

"That was a good trick." Coyote pulled Beaver out of sight, then cleaned up the blood.

"Try it again," Skunk said.

Coyote hurried back to the medicine dance. "My friend was not healed, so your medicine maker set out to find stronger medicine. Will one of you see to my friend now? He is very sick."

"Pick another of us," Beavers said.

Coyote picked the next fattest, then they hurried back. Skunk rolled on the ground, moaning and groaning in pain.

"Where do you hurt?" Beaver asked, leaning over Skunk to get a better look.

Coyote hit the medicine maker over the head, then pulled the body out of sight. He cleaned up the blood and turned to Skunk.

"Would you like another?" Skunk asked.

Coyote loped off to the medicine dance, then picked out another medicine maker. Once back, they pulled the same trick, then a fourth time.

"Thank you," Coyote said. "I believe this is quite enough food."

Skunk quickly ran into the woods.

Coyote carried his game home, proud of his hunt. After all the work, he was hungry. He gave them to his wife.

"Hurry and cook up all this food. I met many friends while I was out today, and I invited them home for a feast."

"That is good," she said.

"After you cook, take the children and leave for a while. Some of my friends will not be looked on by women and children."

"We will do that." She began to prepare the food.

"And do not eat before my friends come because I want to make sure there is enough for all of them."

"We are hungry too, but we will wait to eat," she agreed.

When she finished cooking, she spread out the food for his guests.

Coyote looked it over, nodded in satisfaction, then pointed toward the nearby creek. "While I eat with my guests, take the children over there and do not let them look back."

After they left, Coyote rapped on the door and pretended that people entered the lodge. He talked aloud, pretending to seat his friends in the room.

Satisfied that he had the meat all to himself, he started at one place and ate all the food. He ate from the next and the next, but as he grew less hungry he ate less food from each place.

When he was as full as he could get he pretended to send his friends on their way, laughing and talking and inviting them back. He closed the door, waited awhile, and then called his family home.

"My friends were hungry and enjoyed the food," Coyote said.

"Some of your friends were hungry, but others hardly touched their food," his wife said.

"That is right."

Coyote and his family sat down, and while they ate the leftover meat, he patted his full stomach.

"From now on," he said, "we will move from here and live as coyotes. And there will be such a thing as making feasts for friends."

Coyote Challenges Never-Grows-Larger

One time Ketox, or Coyote, bounded across the prairie and saw Never-Grows-Larger, the smallest snake, sunning on a large, flat rock.

"You are tiny," Coyote said. "I would never want to be as little as you. Look at me. You should be as big as me."

Never-Grows-Larger looked Coyote up and down, then flicked a long, forked tongue out and in.

"Let me see your teeth," Coyote said.

Never-Grows-Larger opened wide to reveal tiny teeth.

"Look at my teeth." Coyote snarled to reveal big, sharp teeth. "With no effort at all I could bite you in two."

Never-Grows-Larger flicked a long tongue out and in again.

"Let us bite each other and see who is more powerful," Coyote said.

"Are you sure?" Never-Grows-Larger asked.

"Yes."

"I accept the challenge."

Coyote bit hard enough to almost sever Never-Grows-Larger's head.

Never-Grows-Larger bit Coyote.

"Now I will go just out of sight, and we will call to each other to see how the other fares." Coyote bounded through the tall grass and lay down out of sight. "Hey!"

"Hey," Never-Grows-Larger called faintly.

"Hey!"

"Hey," Never-Grows-Larger said even more weakly.

Pleased with success, Coyote repeatedly called and listened to Never-Grows-Larger's voice grow soft. "I never doubted I would kill that snake," Coyote whispered.

After a time, Coyote noticed that the snakebite swelled, and the wound started to hurt. "Hey." But the sound was not as loud. Soon Coyote's entire body hurt and swelled up.

"Hey!" Never-Grows-Larger called loud and clear.

"Hey," Coyote said softly.

"Hey!" Never-Grows-Larger called again.

Coyote did not respond.

Never-Grows-Larger crawled through the grass to Coyote's side. The animal lay dead.

Never-Grows-Larger left Coyote there and went back to sunning on the rock.

History

Under a vast sky of bright sunlight and twinkling stars, the Wichita Confederacy arose on the southern plains and prairie. The tribes lived in scattered villages along winding riverbanks, and they hunted on foot and gathered food in rich river valleys. They called themselves Kitikiti'sh, or First People.

One tradition holds that they migrated north from the southeast around the lower Red River, but another suggests that they came from the Wichita Mountains in Oklahoma and moved south.

After the great drought that began in 1350, Wichitas migrated east and south. As they came into closer contact with the Caddo, they adapted corn agriculture and bee-hive-shaped straw houses to their own use. They retained a social system less hierarchical than the Caddo, with their own Caddoan language.

They surrounded their villages with fields of corn, pumpkins, melons, beans, and squash. They made pottery, wooden articles such as vessels and mortars, tools and utensils of stone, and rawhide bags and parfleches.

Straw houses, thirty feet in diameter, were constructed from forked poles covered with dry grass. Around the inside walls nestled platform beds hung with privacy buffalo-hide curtains painted with tribal scenes. Smoke from the center fire rose to the outside through a vent in the roof. Nearby a ten- to twenty-foot square arbor with a raised floor provided a work and rest area during summer heat. Another arbor was used to dry and store meat and vegetables. Young people slept in a thatched hut on a high platform reached with a ladder.

They lived in their villages spring through fall when they planted, tended, and harvested crops. In early winter they left to live in tepees on the annual buffalo hunt. They returned in the spring to start the cycle over again.

In appearance, the Wichita stood shorter in statue than other Plains tribes. They tattooed their faces as well as their bodies. Men tattooed both eyelids with a short horizontal line extending outward from the corners of the eyes. Women tattooed a line down the bridge of the nose to the upper lip, and a line circled the mouth, with four lines extending over the chin. By the mid-nineteenth century, men no longer tattooed their bodies, but women continued the tradition.

Men wore tanned skin breechclouts, leggings in colder weather or for ceremonies, occasionally a deer-leg shirt with fringe, moccasins, and a buffalo robe painted with war or hunt designs. Women wore a tanned buckskin or buffalo-hide wraparound skirt with a poncho. They also wore moccasins, adding leggings and a fur robe in winter. They painted celestial scenes on their clothes and added ornamental rows of elk teeth. By the late nineteenth century, they wore primarily Anglo-American clothes, using a white blanket with a wide colored stripe for a robe.

The Wichita lived in a matriarchal culture. For them, the perfect family consisted of a woman, her husband, unmarried children, daughters and their husbands and children, and her sisters.

As Mother-of-the-House, the oldest competent woman was director of the family unit. When she died, her eldest daughter took her place. She controlled the family, including sons-in-law, even if they were chiefs.

The extended family lived in one house and worked together, and when on the hunt they pitched their tepees near their family group. Close kinship relationships defined their society, so that first cousins were considered brothers and sisters, and a mother's sisters were regarded as mothers. They joked with each other to establish strong ties that lasted lifetimes.

Family cooperation and the good of the community came first in providing for the people. Women tanned, sewed, and painted skins, fenced the fields, cultivated the crops, harvested the produce, and raised the children. Men helped build the houses, plant the crops, and they made bows, arrows, and other utensils. Men hunted for game, but they also spent more time and effort at warfare as their enemies increased from all directions.

Many religious rituals surrounded the birth of children because they were greatly desired and loved. A woman pitched a tepee near her lodge and then a medicine woman helped her give birth inside it. Afterward the medicine woman carried the baby to a nearby stream. Here she cleansed and prayed for the young life, calling on Bright-Shining-Woman and Man-Never-Known-on-

Earth. The father did not enter the mother's lodge for four days after the birth because he might make the mother and child sick.

Children were never harshly disciplined as they learned their place within the tribe. When boys reached a certain age, men took over their training while women continued to train the girls.

At a marriageable age, a young man's family usually sent a member of their group to talk with a young woman's family. If an agreement was reached, the young man's family gave a feast as well as presents of horses and buffalo robes to the bride's father or brother and gifts of fine clothing to the bride. But it was also common not to give feasts or gifts.

After marriage the groom usually joined the bride's family and became responsible for providing fresh meat and herding their horses. He was also expected to build a successful war record. The bride owed his family little, although occasionally she might take a special dish of food to his mother. Her many responsibilities lay with her own family group.

The Wichita practiced elaborate funeral rites. They bathed and dressed the deceased in the finest of clothes and painted the face with personal symbols. They gathered in a cemetery, then buried the dead in a grave with the head to the east and with weapons or other favorite implements. Afterward came a time of purification and mourning for the entire village.

Wichita religion supported a pantheon of gods and goddesses, many located in the stars. Man-Never-Known-on-Earth and Bright-Shining-Woman were especially revered by the people, and they could be petitioned for help. The people also sought guardian spirits through visions, and frequently these came in the guise of animals. They believed that everything in the universe possessed a strong spirit and for that reason should be respected.

Religious celebrations were practiced through song and dance in semisecret religious societies that could be joined by anyone in the tribe. The Deer Dance was held in the spring, summer, and fall to purify and promote health, longevity, and prosperity. Wichita myths, tales of a four-era cycle, were taught to children by an elder who recited them as a prayer.

By the fifteenth century they were part of an established trade route across the Southern Plains. As the central point between Caddo traders in the east and Pueblo traders in the west, they were an important layover and trade center.

As Apaches migrated into the area between 1450 and 1500, they interrupted the established trade network and became enemies of the Wichita and the Caddo. Lipan Apache took over much of the meat-for-corn trade, but the Wichita and Caddo still traded with each other.

In 1542 Spanish conquistador Francisco Coronado reached southern Kansas. He encountered the Kitikiti'sh, or Wichita, a powerful confederacy of seven tribes with a civilization of 30,000 people living in villages that stretched along the Arkansas for twenty-five miles.

Over time the Wichita migrated south, ahead of the Osages and the far-ranging Comanche. They acquired horses from the Pueblos, which gave them more mobility and access to wider territory. Against an increasingly hostile world, they consolidated into larger villages for defense.

By the eighteenth century the Wichita were located

between the Wichita Mountains in Oklahoma and the Brazos and Trinity Rivers of east and central Texas. Five tribes comprised the confederacy: the Taovaya, the Tawakoni, the Wichita, the Yscani or Waco, and the Kichai.

In 1720 the French established an outpost at the Caddo Kadohadacho village on the Great Bend of the Red River, then sent out traders to Wichita villages. Soon the Wichita were part of the French trade network, exchanging horses and deer hides for firearms, ammunition, metal implements, and cloth.

By 1750 two trade networks extended across Texas from French Louisiana: a Caddo-Wichita-Comanche network in the north and an Attakapan-Tonkawa-Apache network in the south. Competition for resources set up a conflict between the two networks, and the tribes raided and fought each other. Access to European manufactured goods changed the tribes' warfare, lifestyle, and culture.

With no immunity to deadly diseases introduced by Europeans, Wichitas lost a great number of people as did all the Indians of Texas. They repeatedly regrouped as epidemics swept through their villages, but when so many died so quickly they lost heritage and culture, friends and family.

The Wichita population numbered 3,200 in 1780. Wichita villages along the upper Red River were susceptible to Osage raids and continual epidemics. They constantly needed to acquire more hides and horses for themselves and for trade. They moved farther south into Texas, combining smaller villages into larger ones for protection.

Outside forces were gathering to bring vast changes to Texas. The United States purchased Louisiana in 1803, and Anglo-Americans poured into the territory. Mexico won its independence in 1821 and then invited Eastern Indians and Anglo-Americans into Texas to gain greater control over the land. Ranchers, planters, and farmers wanted Texas Indians gone. Wichita, a Choctaw term *wia chitoh*, meaning big arbor, first appeared in the Camp Holmes treaty of 1835. Texas won independence from Mexico in 1836 and became a state in 1845. Anglo-Texans insisted that Indians had no rights to any land in Texas.

To protect the Wichita and other Indians who had laid down their arms, the United States government persuaded the Texas legislature in 1854 to establish two Central Texas reservations. Under the direction of Agent Robert S. Neighbors, the Penataka Comanche moved to the Clear Fork Reserve, and Caddos, Tonkawas, Delawares, Shawnees, and Wichita such as the Wacos and Tawakonis moved to the Brazos Reserve.

This did not last long. In 1859 a mob of 300 Anglo-Texans raided the reserves, killed Caddos, and then plotted to exterminate the other Indians.

Agent Neighbors saved the Indians when he led them out of Texas. They left behind houses, crops, livestock, and herds of cattle and horses. Men, women, and children survived temperatures that averaged 106 degrees over a dusty trail of nearly two hundred miles. They arrived with little but their lives at the Wichita and Affiliated Tribes Reservation at Fort Cobb in western Indian Territory. For his efforts, Agent Neighbors was murdered when he returned to Texas.

The Wichita rebuilt their lives, survived the hostilities of the War Between the States, and after the war worked hard to reestablish their reservation. By 1868 the

Wichita numbered 572 people. They continued their traditional way of life by planting crops and hunting game. They also received occasional flour, beef, and cloth distributions from the federal government.

The United States government passed the Dawes Severalty Act of 1887 to break up the reservations. Anglo farmers, ranchers, railroad companies, and oil companies supported it. Texas tribes resisted the Act, and the Kiowa took it to the Supreme Court. They lost.

By 1890 the Wichita population was reduced by eighty-nine percent, and they continued to be subjected to extreme cultural changes. Christian missionaries, teachers, home agents, and government officials with the power to force the Indians from traditional lifestyles descended en masse on the reservations.

In response to these unwanted changes, the Ghost Dance, a spiritual movement that promised Anglo-American removal and a return to traditional culture, swept through many of the Plains tribes in the early 1890s.

In 1895 Congress allotted the Wichita and Affiliated Tribes Reservation. Each Wichita who could prove Indian blood, or Anglo-American man who married an Indian woman, received 160 acres. In a few years many Caddos lost their land to Anglo-Americans, and the majority of the reservation land was opened to settlement.

Again the Wichita rebuilt their lives, continuing to farm and hunt while preserving a great deal of their culture. In 1924 Wichitas, along with other Indians, received United States citizenship. In 1937 they numbered 385 people.

In 1960 the Wichita, Waco, Tawakoni, and Keechi

organized into one government, Wichita and Affiliated Tribes, to become a federally recognized Indian tribe. Despite this, they continued their ancient heritage of sovereignty established long before the existence of the United States.

Today Wichita and Affiliated Tribes have an enrolled membership of over 1,900 people. Many of them live and work in Caddo County, Oklahoma. They continue to provide for their people through tribal programs such as business development, health service, environmental issues, food distribution, social services, and higher education.

They keep their heritage alive through many projects such as Kitikiti'sh Little Sisters, Grass House Building Project, the Wichita Warriors Memorial, and the American Indian Exposition held annually in August at Anadarko, Oklahoma. In the spirit of their ancient matriarchy, each year they elect a Wichita Tribal Princess to represent their nation.

Comanche

This design is based on a Comanche outside shield cover
located in the Smithsonian Institution in Washington, D.C.
The shield is made of yellow-dyed buckskin, with horsehair wrapped
in red cloth, hawk feathers, deer hooves, and an eagle feather.

--- ◆ ---

Myths and Legends

--- ◆ ---

Origin of Days and Seasons

Long ago when darkness and coldness enveloped the Earth, all the animals called a council to discuss the situation. They gathered at a large tepee, then entered to sit in a circle around a brightly burning fire.

"Are you sure you want change?" Coyote asked.

"Yes," Bear growled.

"I want light," Hummingbird said.

"I want heat," Turtle said.

"But change is dangerous." Coyote wanted darkness to cover his mischievous pranks and questionable deeds.

"I like dark," Opossum said.

"My fur coat keeps me warm," Raccoon said.

"We want change," Bear growled.

"I do not need change," Coyote said.

"How can we decide so everyone is satisfied?" Hummingbird asked.

"I know," Coyote said. "Let us play a hand game. Choose sides."

Bear, Turtle, Hummingbird, and others who wanted light and warmth formed a group. Coyote, Raccoon, Opossum, and others who did not want change made up the opposing group.

They sat down across from each other to play. Coyote started the game, but Bear, Turtle, Hummingbird, and their group lost right away. No matter how hard they tried, they could find no way to win.

After another loss, Bear went outside to make strong medicine. When Bear returned, Coyote lost. Now the other group could not win.

Finally Bear stood up, thrust aside the tepee flap, and made a grand gesture toward the outdoors. "Watch. Dawn comes to bring us daylight."

"One more game," Coyote said.

"No," Hummingbird said. "We won."

"Watch my mouth at the break of day," Bear said. "You will see a yellow streak that represents dawn."

"Look in my mouth too," Hummingbird said. "I will show you six tongues to represent warm weather for half the year and cold for the other half.

As dawn broke, casting light over the land, the animals looked in Bear's mouth. They saw a yellow streak.

Hummingbird shouted in triumph, and the animals counted six tongues.

Bear, Turtle, and their group followed Hummingbird outside into the warmth of day.

Coyote and the others huddled inside, frightened.

And that is how day and night, winter and summer came into the world

Spots on the Moon

One time the people camped near a rushing stream. Birds sang in the woods nearby. Horses snorted and pawed the ground. People laughed and talked and worked.

Four children played along the creek. An older girl with a baby in a cradle board on her back joined them. They walked along the meandering stream, straying farther away from the camp as the sun rode across the sky.

A sudden need to move set the people to taking down tepees and striking camp. In a hurry, they did not realize the children were not with them when they left the area.

Sometime later, one of the children played back toward the camp. She saw no tepees, grew frightened, and ran to tell the others.

They could not believe her story and sent another. When that one came back with the same news, they all felt fear. The oldest girl took charge and led them back to camp to pick up the band's trail. They started after their people even though the sun rode low in the west.

Coyote stepped in front of them. "Beware. Big Owl lives near here. Be very quiet, or Peah Moopitz, that giant owl, will hear you."

"Thank you for warning us," the oldest girl said. "We will tread softly and not alert the monster."

Coyote whirled to lope away.

Frightened more than before, they clung together as they continued on the trail.

After awhile the youngest, a little boy, began to cry, tired and hungry and frightened. The others tried to quiet him, but he only wailed louder.

"I hear my nephew. Bring him to me," a voice boomed out from near the stream.

"Uncle!" the little boy said. "I want my uncle."

"I fear that is not your uncle," the oldest girl said. "That may be Big Owl."

"Come here," the voice called again. "Let me care for you."

"My uncle will help us." Tears rolled down the little boy's cheeks.

"I fear Big Owl may eat us," the oldest girl said.

The little boy cried even harder.

"We will go," the oldest girl said. "But we must be careful and run away if Big Owl tries to eat us."

They walked in the direction of the voice, frightened yet determined to get help if possible.

"Right here," the voice boomed out again.

They stepped into a clearing by the stream and saw Big Owl. They shivered in fright at the sight of the hulking monster, but now they were too close to escape. Big Owl could easily overtake them if they ran.

Big Owl soothed them with kind words. "Let the little boy stay with me while you play by the stream. I know how to quiet him."

Afraid to disobey Big Owl, they left the youngest and wandered downstream. Yet they did not go far.

"You are a fine little boy," Big Owl said. "I might keep you always."

"Oh no," he said. "My parents want me back."

"You do as I say, or I will eat you up."

Soon the other children returned, not wanting to leave the youngest too long.

While the oldest girl distracted Big Owl, the boy told the others what Big Owl said to him. Now they feared not only that they might never find their people, but that Big Owl would never let them go. They huddled together, trying to think of a way to escape. At last the oldest girl made a plan, then turned to Big Owl.

"We need to go down the stream to wash the youngest boy and our clothes," she said.

Big Owl thought about it. "Do that, but you may not

go too far. You must answer and return when I call."

"We will do as you say."

They hurried down the stream until they were out of sight of Big Owl, but they still did not know how to escape.

The oldest girl saw a large green frog, and she had another idea. "Frog," she said. "We need help. Big Owl captured us."

"You do need help," Frog said.

"We must find our people's trail before dark. When Big Owl calls, will you reply so we may escape?"

"What do I say?" Frog asked.

"We are still washing," the oldest girl said. "While you say that, we will run away."

"Hurry," Frog said.

The children ran as fast as their legs would take them. They hoped to be far away before Big Owl learned the truth.

"Children," Big Owl called. "Are you finished?"

"We are still washing." Frog imitated the oldest girl's voice.

After a time, Big Owl called again. "I want you children to come back here."

"We are still washing," Frog said.

After calling four times, Big Owl grew suspicious because the answer always sounded the same. Crashing down through the grass to the bank, Big Owl searched for the children everywhere.

"Come back," Big Owl called.

"We are still washing," Frog said.

Big Owl saw the frog. "You tricked me."

"Yes. I got the better of you this time." Frog croaked. "The children ran away a long time ago."

Furious, Big Owl struck out with a big stone club, trying to smash Frog.

Frog leaped into the water and disappeared.

Big Owl roared in anger and ran after the children. Soon they were in sight. "Come back!"

They heard Big Owl, glanced behind, and then ran even harder. They reached a wide river, but they had no way to cross.

Crane stood on the bank, fishing.

"Please help us," the oldest girl cried. "Big Owl chases us."

Crane thought a moment, then picked out a head louse and held it toward the oldest girl. "It will taste bad, but put it in your mouth."

She hesitated.

"If you do, you and the others may use my legs as a bridge across the water."

She put the louse in her mouth.

"Whatever you do," Crane said, "do not spit it out until you are safely on the other side."

The children quickly ran across Crane and reached the far bank of the river. The oldest girl spit out the louse. Still afraid of Big Owl, they hurried on their way.

Big Owl raced up, saw the children getting away, and roared with anger.

"Crane," Big Owl said. "My game escapes. Help me get across."

"If you hold this louse in your mouth, I will let you use my body as a bridge," Crane said. "But do not spit it out until you are on the other side."

Big Owl put the louse inside a great maw, then hurried over Crane. Halfway across, the taste got so bad that Big Owl spit out the louse and fell in the river. Struggling out of the water, Big Owl set out after the children again.

Night darkened the plains, but the children could see by the light of a full moon. They looked back and saw Big Owl again. Now they feared they could never escape.

Nearby, Baby Buffalo grazed on tall grass.

"Will you help?" the oldest girl called. "Big Owl is after us, and we are too tired to run any more."

Baby Buffalo stretched as tall as possible and looked as fierce as possible. "Get behind me and I will try."

"Thank you," the oldest girl said.

The children crowded behind Baby Buffalo and watched Big Owl. Soon the monster came at them, growling and brandishing a stone club.

Baby Buffalo snorted and pawed the ground.

Big Owl laughed. "A baby to protect babies. I will kill and eat you all."

As Big Owl lunged, Baby Buffalo charged and struck hard. Big Owl flew high into the sky, up and up and up toward the bright moon. Soon dark spots appeared across the white surface.

And that is how the spots came to be on the moon.

Deer Medicine

One time the people camped at the base of a mountain near a rushing stream. Over time a person disappeared, then another. The band grew troubled and took their worries to their medicine makers. After sweat lodge purification, after sage and sweet grass cleansing, the medicine makers held council.

"I do not trust those deer," Medicine Man said.

"I trust them less than you." Medicine Woman looked up at the mountain where the deer lived near a large cave.

"I suspect they are stealing our people."

"And keeping them in their cave."

"To eat," Medicine Man said.

"Our people depend on us to care for them."

"And we must do so."

Medicine Man and Medicine Woman walked up the mountain to the cave of the deer.

Guard Deer stood near four sticks at the dark hole of an entrance.

"Good morning," Medicine Woman said. "How are you?"

"You look plump and well," Medicine Man said.

"What food do you eat?" Medicine Woman asked.

"We eat good food," Guard Deer said. "Would you like to see?"

"Yes, we would."

Guard Deer picked up one of the sticks and knocked on the entrance. "One fat buffalo."

A buffalo trotted out.

"That is impressive," Medicine Woman said.

"Watch this." Guard Deer hit the entrance again. "One buffalo calf."

A buffalo calf walked out.

"I am really impressed," Medicine Man said.

"Now you know how we get our food," Guard Deer said. "You may see no more."

"Thank you," Medicine Woman said.

As the medicine makers walked away, they whispered to each other.

"I do not believe that is all in their cave," Medicine

Man said.

"I agree. We must find out what else is in there."

They hid behind a large rock while they considered their problem.

"Maybe we could change the sticks when Guard Deer looks the other way," Medicine Man said.

"Guard Deer is too sharp."

"That is true."

"They must change guards soon and the entrance will be unguarded for a brief time," Medicine Woman said.

"We must strike then."

"Yes."

Without making a sound, they worked their way back to the entrance. Concealed behind rocks and plants, they watched and waited. Soon Guard Deer stepped away to consult the next Guard Deer.

They raced to the entrance.

Medicine Woman grabbed a stick and hit the cave. "Two people."

Two warriors walked out.

Medicine Man placed his hand on the stick, and they struck again. "More men."

Many men ran out of the cave. All of them carried bows with arrows in quivers on their backs.

Deer erupted from all directions, but the warriors fought together to drive them back. When the battle was won by the people, most of the deer lay dead. The medicine makers turned to the deer still alive.

"We are the strongest so hereafter we will eat you," Medicine Man said.

"Your skin and bones, all of your body, will be used to help the people," Medicine Woman added.

Guard Deer raised a head. "So be it."

A Girl's Gift to Her People

In the spring, rain fell from the sky in torrents, flooding the plains. Summer arrived with a fierce heat that baked the land, parching the plants. Fall winds howled down from the north, scouring the earth clean. Winter swept in with a chill so cold that ice covered the ground even to the woodlands along the coast. Finally spring returned, but it brought a great drought that spread across the land.

Children cried with hunger. Hunters stalked after game but returned empty-handed. Mothers boiled rawhide for soup. Disease swept through the camps. Misery piled upon misery. The people danced, the drums pounded, but nothing changed. Finally they admitted that the Great Spirit must be displeased with them, so they turned to their medicine makers for help.

That night Medicine Man went up on a sacred hill to make council with the Great Spirit, offering sweet grass and sage. The people waited.

One young girl called She-Who-Is-Alone watched the hill all night long, clutching her doll to her thin chest. She did not want to lose any more of the people to hunger or disease. Her parents already lay dead. She never knew her grandparents. Now she had only her cornhusk doll, made by her mother and decorated by her father.

She stroked her doll, touching the soft white doeskin, the black hair from a horse's tail, and the beautiful blue feathers of the bird who calls, "Jay, Jay." Nothing in all the world mattered more to her than this doll who was both friend and family.

"Do not be afraid," she said to the doll. "You are safe with me and the people."

She waited with all the others as the sun rose, then set and rose again. Finally the next day a crier ran through the village, telling everyone that Medicine Man was coming down from the hill.

The people gathered in a circle around Medicine Man. She-Who-Is-Alone sat to one side, stroking her doll as she watched and listened.

Medicine Man smoked the sacred pipe, holding it up in offering to Father Sky, down to Mother Earth, then to the Four Sacred Directions. "A vision blessed me. Great Spirit believes we are selfish, taking more from Mother Earth than we return. Our troubles are a warning to change our ways."

The people muttered in fear, and She-Who-Is-Alone clasped her doll close for comfort.

"The Great Spirit asks that we make a sacrifice to show our remorse," Medicine Man said. "We must select our most prized possession as a sacrifice, then burn it and cast the ashes to the four winds. When this is done, Mother Earth will nourish us once more."

She-Who-Is-Alone hugged her doll, then sang and danced with her people around the council fire.

Later the people discussed what they must offer to the Great Spirit. First one and then another objected to sacrificing a favorite bow or robe or tepee cover. No one could agree. They argued until they sought the warmth of their tepees that night.

She-Who-Is-Alone lay awake, clutching her doll tightly to her chest. She knew what must be done. She did not want others to grieve as she did for her parents. She walked outside, carrying her doll, and made her way to the council fire that burned low.

"You are my most precious possession," she said to her

doll. "I love you as I love my parents." A tear ran down her cheek. "Surely the Great Spirit wants you."

She picked up a burning stick from the council fire, then walked quietly from the camp. On top of the hill where Medicine Man spoke with the Great Spirit, she gathered twigs and built a fire.

Stroking her doll, she looked up to see a full moon and bright stars in the dark sky. "Great Spirit, take my doll so my people may live."

She kissed her doll a final time. "You will be safe in the spirit world, and I will join you some day."

She gently placed her sacrifice in the fire and then watched her doll burn to ashes, the blue feathers consumed last. When the ashes cooled, she scooped them into her small hands, then cast them to the east, the south, the west, and the north. Exhausted, she could do no more. She lay down and soon fell asleep.

She-Who-Is-Alone awoke to feel the warmth of the sun on her face the next morning. She remembered her sacrifice. As she stood up, she grieved for the loss of her doll, but her grief turned to joy as she looked around at the land.

In all four directions where she had cast the ashes, she saw a blanket of beautiful flowers the exact shade of blue as the bird who calls, "Jay, Jay."

When she came down from the sacred hill to share the wonder with her people, a gentle rain fell from the sky. The people came out of their tepees and looked about in wonder.

The medicine makers called a council to announce that all would now be well because of the sacrifice of She-Who-Is-Alone. They held a celebration in honor of the girl, and she received many gifts. Medicine Man gave her a new name.

She-Who-Dearly-Loves-Her-People.

And since that day, the Great Spirit honors her sacrifice by blanketing the people's land in the spring with flowers the color of the bird who calls, "Jay, Jay."

Two Buffalo Speak

Soko Wechki, or Land Searcher, selected nine warriors to go with him on a raid for horses. They left their village, then set out south. After they traveled awhile, they made camp at a certain place to rest. Soon they noticed two buffalo running on a narrow trail nearby, a large one followed by a smaller one.

"We need food," Land Searcher said.

All the warriors agreed.

Land Searcher looked over the men. Each warrior in every band specialized in a particular area, so he selected the warrior who was the best buffalo hunter.

"Buffalo Hunter, go over and kill one of those buffalo for food."

Buffalo Hunter went after his prey, making no sound, disturbing no rock or plant. He stayed hidden from view as he crawled close to the trail. Once he was in shooting distance, he waited for the buffalo to pass near him. Soon he heard voices coming from the trail.

"Noomah'rah, Brother-in-law, what is the name of the river we near?"

"Surely you recognize this river," a deeper voice

responded.

"No, I do not remember the river."

"North Canadian. A little creek called Peah Quasi Honovit, Big Beaver River, joins it from the north."

"Yes, I remember now."

"You should not forget. That is sweet, clear water, and our people cannot live without it."

Buffalo Hunter watched the buffalo pass without notching an arrow, then he hurried back to camp.

"Why did you not shoot a buffalo?" Land Searcher asked. "We are hungry."

"Those buffalo are powerful medicine. They speak our language."

All the warriors leaned forward to learn more.

"They named the rivers North Canadian and Big Beaver. Their power kept me from shooting them."

Land Searcher looked around at the warriors. "Buffalo medicine is powerful. We will always call the rivers by their buffalo names."

Comanche Captive

Long ago Comanches on the warpath fought the Osage, their bitter enemy. During the fight, a boy was captured and taken back to Osage country.

When the Comanche warriors returned home without the boy, there was much weeping and wailing in the village. Mother, father, and sister grieved so hard that the sister's husband decided to rescue her young brother.

Noomah'rah, or Brother-in-law, called on two brave warriors to help him, and they set out after the Osage.

After riding long and hard, they reached the Osage camp. They ground-tied their horses, then waited for dark in the brush where they could not be seen.

When night finally descended to mask their movements, Brother-in-law prepared to steal into camp.

"Wait here." He gestured to the other warriors. "Watch the horses and be ready to ambush."

They clutched their bows.

"I will try to find him."

In the Osage camp, the Comanche boy was tied on top of a *herkee*, a brush arbor frame made of poles. His feet and palms were slashed. All afternoon long he lay bound under the burning rays of the sun, receiving no food or water, and his blood ran down to mix with the earth.

As he endured the pain, he listened to the Osage make ready for a great war dance. A strong, steady drum beat filled the air. Flames licked upward from the woodpile directly under him. He prayed he would die swiftly and well.

Under cover of the Osage victory dance, Brother-in-law crept close to the fire, but he did not see the boy. He heard groans above his head and looked up. Flickering firelight illuminated a still body.

"Is that you, my wife's brother?"

"Yes." The boy's voice was faint from weakness. "Do not try to save me, or you may be caught. Let my sister cry for only one of us."

"I will not leave you."

"You must. Do not worry. I will die before they come for me again."

"Take heart. My horse is near and I will take you

home. Your sister will cry no more tears."

The boy was too weak to respond.

"Do you hear?"

A muffled groan came from above.

Brother-in-law glanced about the camp. Osages danced hard and fast as their celebration reached its peak. They showed no interest in the captive tied to the *herkee*. He hoped they had forgotten about the boy. He slipped from camp, then came back with a horse and one warrior. He cut the ropes that bound his brother-in-law, then he tied him to the back of the horse because he was too weak to ride. They crept away from the camp, mounted their horses, and rode for home.

When they reached their village, everyone praised them. During the victory dance, the boy's father gave his son-in-law a fine horse in appreciation.

ᕴᛣ•ᐟ〜〜ᛣᕱ

Nuahnuh's Moccasins

On a sunny summer afternoon, Nuahnuh carried water back from the stream. Smoke curled lazily upward from tepees, creating a smoky haze above the village. She watched children play, elders sew hides, and warriors make arrows.

As she walked, she felt the soft slide of buckskin across her skin. She was proud of her new three-skin dress decorated with bright paint and fringe. She also wore new moccasins, a gift from her husband's mother. She was taking special care not to dirty any of her fine new clothes.

As she neared her own tepee, she heard surprised shouts followed by a rain of arrows.

"Osage attack!" the chief yelled. "Get to cover."

She glanced around and saw that the horses tied near camp in case of a surprise attack were gone, silently released and driven away. The scouts who should have warned them must be dead. Soon she would be too if she did not get out of camp.

Dropping the water, she ran after the others, but an arrow caught her in the shoulder. She staggered, then went down. In the confusion of the fight, the Osages ran over her, driving her into the ground. She lay as if dead, her only defense now, as she listened to her people die around her.

She felt blood running from her wound, ruining her beautiful new clothes. She consoled herself that soon she would not care.

Slowly the sounds of fight died down, the moans of pain ceased, and quiet swept across the ruins of the village. She waited, pretending to be dead until night blanketed her in darkness with only moonlight to illuminate the carnage around her.

Nuahnuh raised her head. The Osage were gone. She wanted to be far away in case they came back. Weak from loss of blood, she pulled her body along on the ground with one hand. Now her new buckskin would be dirty as well as bloody, but she still lived.

After a time she grew too weak to continue. She lay her head against the warm earth for a moment.

"My friend." A woman knelt beside Nuahnuh, then picked up her foot and slipped off a moccasin. "You are dead and gone. I am sorry. I lost my moccasins in the fight. I need yours and you need them no more."

Nuahnuh recognized the language of her people and raised her head. "Do not feel pity for me."

The woman yelped in surprise and dropped Nuahnuh's foot.

"I am far from dead. I pretended to be dead in case you were an Osage returned to strip the dead."

"I am Comanche as much as you."

"My friend, you may have my moccasins if you will see I am safely carried from here to my people."

"Keep your moccasins. Many of us still live. We are taking the wounded to a new camp."

"Please wear my moccasins. You will walk far while I must be carried."

As the woman put on the moccasins, Nuahnuh smiled. "I only ask that you try to keep them clean."

Horse Raid

Under a full moon, Comanche warriors rode out on a raid into Mexico to steal horses. These animals were their lifeblood, essential to move camp, hunt buffalo, catch prairie chickens, play games, steal other horses, and fight enemies.

Such an important and dangerous mission left nothing to chance. After scouts found a suitable horse herd, warriors made detailed plans to be strictly followed by each warrior on the raid.

This night the warriors followed directions exactly to

reach a certain point. They stopped.

Usually horses kept on the range needed only one guard or soldier. If the guard held the lead mare by a long rope, he could control the entire herd because they would follow the leader.

Only one warrior advanced toward the horse herd. He moved without sound, aware that any mistake on his part would alert the herd and alarm all the guards. Soon not only would he be dead, but the entire war party as well.

He crept silently up to the guard. The young man slept on duty. Without making a sound the warrior found the rope, then cut it halfway between the leader and the guard. He led the mare without making a sound, and the other horses followed closely behind.

Safely away, the other warriors joined him. They each caught a horse and then galloped toward home.

Ghost Warrior

Once long ago Ehkap-tuh, a warrior named Red, went on the warpath with friends and relatives. After riding across the plains on a long, hot day, they made camp near a hidden spring.

While they rested, enemy warriors attacked. Caught by surprise, several warriors fell to arrows, wounded or dead. Everyone else ran for cover as they scattered in all directions. The enemies stole horses, even Red's favorite war horse.

When the fighting ended, Red was on foot, alone,

hungry, tired, and lost. He thought about his friends, wondering who lived and who died. He needed to get back to his people, so he set out on foot.

Soon night drove away the day, but he kept up his steady pace. After a time he sensed somebody behind him. He feared the enemy warriors tracked him. He looked back, but he saw no one. He continued onward, but the feeling grew. He glanced back again. This time he saw a horse and rider silhouetted against the evening sky.

He tensed for an attack, but he kept on his way. He glanced back again. The stranger paced behind him. He stopped. The warrior stopped too. He walked and the stranger followed, keeping the same distance.

Even strong and experienced warriors could fear the unknown, and he did. Tired, discouraged, and afraid, he reached the timberline. He stepped into the shadows of the trees and felt safe for he could hide there. He sat down under an ancient oak, so tired he could not stay awake a moment longer.

He dreamed Puch'ta-yi, a ghost, rode close and made the sign for the Comanche with his hand.

"I followed you to help, but your fear kept me at a distance," the ghost warrior said.

"At dawn walk east until you reach a creek. Bathe in the water until you cleanse away the past. Walk east again until you reach a hill. On the other side is a herd of horses. One awaits your touch."

And the ghost warrior rode away.

At dawn Red awoke and remembered his dream. He broke camp and walked east. He brought his vision to life up to the moment he looked out over the herd of horses. He called. One raised a noble head, tossed a long mane, and trotted over to him. He vaulted onto the horse's back and headed home.

This time he had no stolen horses to bring his people, but he returned with a powerful vision from a ghost.

Big Owl

Peah Moopitz, or Big Owl, plagued the people year after year. They endured attacks, they paid tribute in buffalo meat, they hunted with trap, arrow, lance, but nothing stopped Peah Moopitz.

One day Big Owl sat under an ancient cottonwood tree as a storm blew in from the north. Dark clouds turned the day to night. Lightning flashed. Thunder rumbled. Peah Moopitz hooted in delight, enjoying the beauty of wild weather.

Suddenly a lightning bolt flashed down and struck the cottonwood tree. Thunder cracked. The tree burst into flames, then disappeared in a haze of smoke.

When the smoke cleared, a small owl hopped from the ashes, blinking in surprise.

Otter and Fox Hospitality

Otter and his family lived in a snug home on the bank of a creek. They seldom had visitors, but with so many children they rarely noticed.

One day Fox trotted up. "Good day, Brother-in-law. I did not realize you lived here."

"We have made this our home for a long time."

"A very nice place."

"Rest here a moment," Otter said. "We do not have food today, but let me talk with my wife."

Otter went inside.

"Fox is known to visit people when it is time to eat," Otter's wife said. "But we have nothing to offer."

Otter sighed. "To be polite we must let him eat one of our children."

"Yes, it is the only right thing to do."

Otter and his wife walked outside. They called their children to stop swimming in the creek and come to the bank.

"Fox, you may eat the plumpest one," Otter said. "Make your choice."

Surprised, Fox looked them over, then picked out the fattest.

Otter killed the little one, then he cleaned, cooked, and served the small otter. "You may eat the meat, but you must save the bones."

Fox nodded in agreement as he greedily bit into the meat and ate right down to the bones.

When Fox finished, Otter's wife collected the bones and then tossed them into the creek. When the bones hit the water, the little one returned to life and swam through the water.

Fox watched in amazement. "Thank you for the meal. I make my home up the creek where the water is deep. Visit me anytime."

After Fox left, the Otter family jumped into the stream and played in the water.

Sometime later Otter swam upstream and noticed Fox in the willow trees along the bank. He stepped out of the water for a visit.

"Good day, Brother-in-law," Otter said.

Fox saw Otter on the bank and motioned to his little ones. "Jump in the stream and swim."

Surprised, the children splashed into the water and started to play.

Otter walked up to Fox. "You have a nice place here."

"Thank you. It is good of you to visit. We are short of food, but my wife and I will think of something for you."

Fox called his wife outside and his children in from the creek. He pointed at the young ones, then looked at Otter. "Pick out the one you want to eat."

Otter looked them over and selected the plumpest one.

Fox killed the little one, then he cleaned and cooked the small fox. He handed the meal to Otter.

"Enjoy the meat, but do not eat the bones." Fox repeated the words Otter had spoken to him.

Otter ate the meat but left the bones.

Fox tossed the bones into the creek, then he stood on the bank waiting for his little one to swim to the surface. Fish fought over the bones, but the young fox never surfaced again.

Fox and Owl Juggle Eyes

One day Ka'wash, or Fox, visited Owl.

"Brother-in-law, would you teach me a trick? I would like to be a magician," Fox said.

"I know many tricks," Owl said. "I will show you one, but you must do exactly as I say."

"I would think of nothing else," Fox said.

"Let me show you a trick."

Owl removed a large eye and threw it high into a willow tree, then he took out the other eye and tossed it up after the first one.

Fox watched in amazement.

"Eyes fall!" Owl's eyes fell back into their sockets, then Owl performed the trick three more times.

"That is a most impressive," Fox said. "Let me try."

"Are you sure you understand?"

"Yes." Fox pulled out an eye and tossed it up into the willow, then did the same with the other.

"Do you remember what to say?"

"Eyes fall!" Fox's eyes fell back into their sockets.

"That is good," Owl said. "You may perform this trick as long as you follow two rules."

"Rules?"

"Yes. Never toss your eyes more than four times a day, and you must always throw them into a willow tree."

"I will not forget."

Fox trotted away, thinking and talking of this great new power.

"I am a magician. Others will be most impressed. This is such a great trick I believe I will perform it all day long. And why should I go to the trouble of finding a willow tree? Owl may be smart, but not that smart."

At the first willow tree, Fox tossed up one eye then the other. "Eyes fall!" When the eyes landed back in their sockets, Fox continued down the trail, stopping at two more willows to perform the same trick.

Fox stopped under an elm. "This trick works so well that the tree will not matter." First one eye went up, then the other.

"I will prove that I am a stronger magician than Owl. Eyes fall!"

Nothing happened.

"Eyes fall!"

Still nothing happened. No matter how many times Fox called, the eyes did not return.

Turtle Challenges Rabbit to a Race

Rabbit roasted three fat prairie dogs in the hot coals of a big fire. A delicious aroma filled the air, making Rabbit's stomach growl. Anxious to eat after a hard day's hunt, Rabbit waited impatiently for the prairie dogs to cook.

"Hello, Brother-in-law." Turtle said, as he strolled up, then glanced around Rabbit's camp. "You look busy."

"That I am," Rabbit said.

"What do I smell?" Turtle asked.

"Plump prairie dogs."

"I propose a race."

Rabbit chuckled. "Why? You cannot win against me."

"If we want to make it fair, I need a head start."

"You will still be too slow. I can win with a rock tied to one foot."

"You could take a nap while I get started."

"I can take several naps and still beat you," Rabbit said.

"Let us begin on the other side of the hill and race back. The winner gets to eat the prairie dogs."

Rabbit laughed again. "I suppose that will give me something to do while I wait for my food to cook."

They took their time going over the hill, then Rabbit sat down and leaned against a tree.

Turtle started back, moving as quickly as possible.

Rabbit yawned, feeling the weight of the day, and dozed without meaning to sleep.

Turtle kept steadily walking but glanced back in worry. Rabbit could catch up at any moment. Soon the aroma of cooking food filled the air. Turtle walked harder, tired as well as hungry now. Finally Turtle reached the prairie dogs and sat down to eat. Smacking and gobbling, Turtle kept watch for Rabbit.

As the last bite slid down Turtle's throat, Rabbit raced up. "You tricked me!"

"You slept too long."

"I was tired from hunting and cooking the prairie dogs."

Turtle got up. "You are a good cook."

Rabbit kicked at the coals. "That is not fair."

"You agreed to the race." Turtle laughed. "Thank you for the delicious meal." Heavy and full from the prairie dogs, Turtle slowly crept away.

Coyote Girl

One day a mother realized she needed more water to cook so she turned to her young daughter.

"We are camped far from the stream, so let us ride over there. You may play while I get water."

"I will take my doll."

"And I will bring food."

They laughed together as they packed their horses, then headed out of camp, not realizing that a man followed them.

At the creek, the mother left her daughter to watch the horses and play while she walked downstream.

The man tracked the mother and caught her by surprise. He insulted her, then grabbed her. She fought back, but he overpowered her, finally choking her.

He crept back to the daughter and surprised her as well. He made her mount her mother's horse, then they rode far away from the stream.

Finally he stopped and jerked the girl from the horse. He killed her mother's horse, then abandoned the girl alone with nothing except what she wore.

At the camp, the girl's people worried about her. After a time they grieved for her, hoping she would some day find her way home.

The girl learned to survive alone as she made her way across the plains and then to a stream. She saw no people, but she made friends with many animals.

She liked coyotes best, and one adopted her. This coyote guarded her so she would not be hurt. Time passed. Her hair grew longer, her skin turned dark and tough, and she moved, acted, and looked much like an animal. Happy now, her past a dim memory, she lived the free life of the coyote.

One day when her guardian coyote was away, the other coyotes of their band held a council. They agreed the girl must go back to her true people. They knew the way. Yet they realized her guardian would object, so they decided to do it that very day. They went to the den and found her.

"You must return to your own people," a leader said.

"No," the girl said. "I like it here. And my guardian would not want me to leave."

"Your guardian is gone," another coyote said.

"We must take her away now," a coyote said.

"Please let me live here," she said.

But the coyotes refused to listen to her, for they believed they knew best.

Many days later and far away from the coyote camp, people in a village near a creek worked and played. At dusk several of them saw a pack of dogs appear on a hill in the west. The pack traveled toward the village, then stopped to lay down an object. People gathered to watch the strange sight. When the pack turned to leave, the people realized they watched coyotes.

Eight warriors with bows and arrows ran to see what the coyotes left. They found a terrified creature who looked part animal and part girl. They took her back to camp. Despite her wild appearance, her family recognized her and welcomed her with love.

Yet her family grew sad because Coyote Girl could never be completely happy with her people. She always longed to run with the coyotes.

---◆---

History

---◆---

Under the light of a full moon, Comanche warriors in full regalia rode across Comanchería, a heart-shaped area that covered over 250,000 miles of hills and mountains, plains and rivers. From the Arkansas River in Colorado and Kansas to the Guadalupe River in Texas, from the Sangre de Cristo Mountains in New Mexico to the Cross Timbers in Texas, a full moon came to mean Comanche Moon.

Anyone who traveled into Comanchería, much less put down roots there, without invitation from a Comanche band became fair game just as much as the buffalo. It was war. The might of the Spanish army, the Mexican army, the Texan army, the Texas Rangers, and finally the United States army could not defeat the Comanche cavalry. In one battle alone, the kill ratio was three Comanches to six hundred soldiers.

Anglo-Americans were not the first to collide with the Comanche. Utes, Pawnees, Osages, Tonkawas, Apaches, and Navajos all gave way as the Comanche carved out a country and then defended it from outside aggression.

The Comanchería originally consisted of thirteen regional divisions made up of independent bands, but by the middle of the nineteenth century only half that number were known to exist.

The Southern Comanche division was the Penateka, Honey Eaters. The Middle Comanche divisions consisted of the Tenawa, Those-Who-Stay-Downstream; the Nokoni, Wanderers; the Kotosteka, Buffalo Eaters; and the Quahada, Antelopes, in the west. The Northern Comanche division was the Yamparika, Root Eaters.

Yet long before the existence of the Comanchería, Eastern Shoshone groups lived near the upper Platte River in eastern Wyoming and the mountains of Montana. They developed their culture from a harsh environment, and around the beginning of the sixteenth century, several bands spread onto the northern Plains to hunt buffalo on foot. Difficult and dangerous, this task required the expertise of all members of a band, including women and children. It also set them in conflict with Crow, Blackfoot, and Plains Apache.

After the Pueblo revolt against the Spanish in 1680, many Shoshone bands acquired horses. They no longer needed to use dogs as domestic transportation. Horses set them free to migrate in search of more horses and other land. On their way south, they fought the Utes, who named them Kohmahts, Those-Who-Are-Against-Us, and the Spanish changed it to Comanche. They called themselves Nümü, the People, even as they continued to speak Shoshonean of the Uto-Aztecan language family.

In 1740 the Comanche traded for firearms with the French and soon established themselves as Lords of the Southern Plains. They were unmatched on horseback and as warriors, but they also excelled in trade, becoming part of the Comanche-Wichita-Caddo trade network.

Comanches trained horses, but more important they were one of the few tribes to breed them. They specialized in fast paints and pintos. Soon French, Spanish, and Americans bought and traded for Comanche horses. Other tribes sometimes stole horses because the Comanche were such tough traders. It caused war. The

Comanche always retaliated for any transgression against them, and this put them in constant conflict.

In time the horse became the measure of wealth in the Comanche bands, and a single warrior might claim up to 3,000 horses. In order to ensure enough grass for their enormous horse herds, Comanches sometimes moved their villages every eight to ten days. They usually camped near streams where they had access to a good water supply, and their tepees might stretch for miles along the water.

The Comanche never had enough horses or enough children. Women gave birth to usually one or at most two or three children during their lifetime, and many men died young. This shortage sent warriors on raids as far as a thousand miles into Mexico and as far north as Saskatchewan. They stole horses, but they also captured women and children. The women were ransomed or traded while the children were adopted and treated as full members of the band. Once raised as a Comanche, most never left.

Independent in mind, spirit, and body, the Comanche warrior answered to no one, not even a god. If a warrior decided to lead a war party, he would invite other warriors to his lodge. After explaining his mission, he would pass around a pipe. Those who believed in his medicine and wanted to go, smoked the pipe, but those who let it pass did so with no stigma.

In time a warrior who showed consistent courage, success, restraint, and wisdom might become a war chief or even a head war chief of a band or a division, but his power was strictly limited to the force of his personality and prestige. A council of the men had to reach consensus for any decision to be put into effect. Women and children did not sit in council, but women influenced all decisions.

The Comanche believed in Sky Father and Earth Mother, as well as the Sacred Directions of the Earth, but they also thought the Great Spirit usually had little interest in their affairs. They always gave thanks for the bounty they received from the land, and they joined medicine societies.

Young men went on vision quests to obtain the personal power that would guide them through their lives, and they might also go again as the need arose. Their supernatural guardian could appear as a buffalo, bear, eagle, beaver, or other animal.

Boys learned the art of warrior and hunter, making bows and arrows, lances, shields, and saddles. They became expert riders with the ability to shoot five arrows in succession from under a racing horse's neck while holding on with their legs.

Girls worked just as hard to master the difficult tasks of creating everything the tribe needed to survive. Hunters brought in buffalo, or deer and antelope. Girls and women, with some help from boys and men, tanned the hides, then made them into clothes, tepee covers, and utensils. They also gathered firewood and water, as well as much of the food such as chokecherries, pecans, plums, and wild potatoes to make bread and stew. They made pemmican from ground dried buffalo meat mixed with fat and salt. They learned which herbs, roots, and cactus to use for medicine. They made many products that later were traded for firearms, metal, fabric, and other items.

Highly valued, women were the backbone of the bands, giving birth to the children, training them, tending the fires when the men were at war. As women aged they gained more power, respect, freedom, and many became medicine makers. Male elders were expected to act in a manner opposite to the young warriors, becoming gentle and patient as they taught the young.

The Comanche differed from other Plains tribes in several ways. Their tepees used a framework of four poles like the Shoshone instead of three poles. Some warriors wore a war bonnet made from a buffalo scalp with horns, not adopting the long feathered bonnet until much later. And the Comanche divisions did not gather together each summer.

Comanches enjoyed storytellers. They played games such as horseracing, arrow-shooting, foot-racing, stick-ball, hoop, and a hand game of sticks. They liked to sing and dance, creating the Buffalo Dance, Gift Dance, Crow Dance, War Dance, and Round Dance.

Usually the men wore a leather belt with a buckskin breechclout, close-fitting deerskin leggings tied to their belt, and moccasins with tough buffalo hide soles and soft deerskin uppers. In winter they added a heavy buffalo robe and buffalo-hide boots. Later they liked to wear blue and red wool trade blankets. In the nineteenth century they added buckskin shirts. They wore their hair in two long braids wrapped with thongs or beaver fur and tied a single feather to a scalp lock. Several earrings dangled from each ear, and they might paint and tattoo their faces and bodies.

Women cut their hair to shoulder length when they married, then gave their hair to their husbands who added it to their braids. They wore soft three-skin dresses dyed in colors and edged with fringe. Later they added beads and metal in favorite designs of zigzag, arrow, crossed arrows, or cactus flower. They wore moccasins and leggings. Women might also tattoo and paint their bodies. They liked to paint the inside of their ears bright red, paint orange and red circles on their cheeks, and outline their eyes with red and yellow.

Normally two or three women, sometimes sisters, married one man because women always outnumbered the men due to constant warfare. Each woman had her own tepee, but they shared child-rearing responsibilities. They usually married within their own band, otherwise the wife most often went to live with her husband's family.

A man courted the woman of his choice, and her brother or father as well, so that when he brought a horse or important item to her tepee to show how much he valued this chosen woman, he usually knew that his suit would be accepted.

Children were greatly valued and loved, never experiencing any type of chastisement beyond a stern lecture. Elders were also loved and valued for their wisdom and their contribution to the band. Men and women cried and grieved over the death of a loved one, and women might slash their arms to show their pain. Warriors never left a downed friend on the battlefield, and they risked their own lives to bring home the dead.

Free and powerful in the Comanchería, the Nümü never anticipated an enemy they could not fight. In 1781 Anglo-Americans brought a new type of war. Smallpox. The Comanche had no natural immunity or medicine to fight it, and many of the people quickly died.

They continued to live as before, defending the Comanchería from other tribes, trading horses, and raising children. In 1805 they made a peace with the Kiowa that has never been broken.

In 1816 smallpox again swept through the Comanchería, killing many more. They recovered to go forward, dealing now with the new independent Mexico instead of Spain.

The United States government destabilized the area in the early nineteenth century with a relocation policy. Tribes east of the Mississippi River were moved to Kansas and Indian Territory. These Indians hunted west onto the Comanchería, and for the first time Anglo-Americans had trouble with the Comanche.

Texas won independence from Mexico in 1836, but Anglo-Texans refused to stay off designated Indian land. They demanded Indian removal or extermination. Comanches fought back. The Texas Rangers were, in large part, formed to subdue them.

In 1840 some Penetaka Comanches after years of war asked for a peace council in order to set a boundary between Anglo-Texans and Indians. They were invited to San Antonio. Twelve chiefs along with fifty-three men, women, and children arrived for council. Anglo-Texans attacked, killing thirty Comanches, which included most of the chiefs, three women, and two children. They took the others captive. Seven Anglo-Texans died in the Council House Fight.

When other Comanches learned of the betrayal, a war party made a thousand-mile raid through Texas, burning homes and killing hundreds of settlers.

The Republic of Texas became the State of Texas in 1845, and the United States government established a string of forts in an attempt to ring Comanchería. War continued, but the Comanche had limited numbers of people while the Anglo-Americans were without end. In 1849 the California gold rush drew Anglo-American miners west, and they brought smallpox to the Canadian River. An epidemic broke out, and by 1851 the Comanche dropped in number from 20,000 to 12,000. In 1854 the Texas legislature finally agreed to two Indian reservations in Central Texas. The Penataka Comanche moved to Clear Fork Reserve, and other Indians went to the Brazos Reserve. Anglo-Texans repeatedly attacked the reservations. A Trail of Tears to Indian Territory in 1859 saved the Indians from extermination, but they had to abandon all land and property in Texas.

Confederate leaders broke their treaties with the Comanche in 1861, so Comanches pushed the Texas frontier back a hundred miles. By 1863 the hostility of Union soldiers on the frontier forged an alliance of the Comanche, Lakota, Cheyenne, Arapaho, Kiowa, and Kiowa-Apache. At the end of the War Between the States, the Santa Fe and Overland Trails were closed, and the Plains tribes were at war with the United States. Government commissioners soon met with the tribes to arrange peace.

In 1867 Anglo-American hunters started the slaughter of buffalo, the Plains tribes' primary food source, with free ammunition issued by army commanders. To save their people, the Treaty of Medicine Lodge was signed by all the Comanche divisions except the Quahada of West Texas, who had an outbreak of cholera in their camps and did not attend. The Comanche and the Kiowa exchanged the Comanchería for a three-million-acre reservation in southwest Indian Territory.

The Comanches moved near Fort Cobb, but no food was provided for them as specified in their treaty so they raided in Texas that summer. The army hounded them and ordered them to return. Soon they were resettled at Fort Sill, the new location for the Comanche-Kiowa agency.

By 1870 the Comanche population was estimated at 8,000, and only the Quahada remained free on the Staked Plains. All the other Plains tribes were on reservations. In 1874 the Comanche agent's census listed 2,643 Comanches on the reservation.

Unable to defeat, capture, or kill the Quahada, in 1875 United States army troops, Texas Rangers, and Tonkawa scouts descended on the Palo Duro Canyon. They drove off the warriors, burned five villages with winter food supplies, massacred women and children, and slaughtered 2,000 horses. They relentlessly pursued the starving survivors throughout the winter.

The Quahada fought sixteen battles with the army from that time to the spring of 1875. They won them all. Finally they learned that an official army order had been issued for the Quahada to submit to the reservation or be exterminated. With the land and food gone, women, children, and elders in need, Chief Quanah Parker led the last 600 Comanches to Fort Sill. By that summer the war was over.

Anglo-Americans had won the Comanchería, but at a terrible cost in human life. Only 1,597 Comanches remained alive.

In 1879 the great herds of buffalo that roamed the Plains were gone too. In ten years, Anglo-American hunters exterminated fifteen million buffalo. At one point, sickened by the slaughter, the Texas legislature decided to pass a law against the carnage, but the United States army persuaded it that Anglo-Americans needed the buffalo dead so Indian tribes could not hunt for food and the Plains could be plowed by settlers. The law did not pass, and only an estimated 1,500 buffalo survived.

On their reservation north of the Red River, the Comanche collected tolls on cattle herds crossing their land and leased their grasslands to Texas cattle ranchers. They continued to speak their own language and live traditional lives, but they were under tremendous pressure from the United States government to give up their heritage. Soon missionaries and teachers arrived, determined to turn the Comanche into Christian Americans.

In 1901 Comanches were forced to give up their tribal reservation. Under the Jerome Agreement, each man, woman, and child received 160 acres. The Comanche allotments totaled less than ten percent of the three million acres guaranteed by the Medicine Lodge Treaty. With the other ninety percent, the last great Anglo-American land rush was held on Commanchería.

In 1916 Comanche warriors volunteered for service in World War I. Comanche code talkers were invaluable to the United States armed forces, because the German army could not translate their language.

In 1924 Comanches, along with other Indians, received United States citizenship.

Comanche warriors volunteered in 1941 to serve the United States in World War II. Code talkers used the Comanche language in the D-Day Invasion and Patton's tank battalion to gain victory for the allied forces.

In 1967 the Comanche Nation adopted a formal constitution.

The French government awarded their highest honor, Chevalier de L'Order National du Merite, in 1989 to Comanche warriors for their important contribution to freedom in World War II as code talkers.

In 1994 the Comanche Nation adopted an official alphabet for their spoken language, and Nümü Tekwapüha Nomneekatü was formed to preserve Comanche culture.

Comanches officially opened the Comanche Veteran's Memorial in Lawton, Oklahoma, in 1995 to honor the Comanche veterans of World War I, World War II, Korea, and Vietnam.

In 1996 the enrolled population of the Comanche Nation reached 10,000, and they continued their tribal traditions.

Nümü, the people, still live and thrive in Commanchería.

Alabama-Coushatta

This design is based on an Alabama incised pottery
motif of Thunderbirds.

---◆---

Myths and Legends

---◆---

Origin of the Alabama and Coushatta

A long time ago the Alabama and Coushatta arose from the clay of the Earth deep inside a cave. They lived in darkness. One day they noticed Ground Hog dig upward. They decided to follow. Up and up they went, but they tired and camped three times to rest along the way.

At last they arrived at the mouth of the huge cave. An ancient tree's roots snaked down deep into the soil. The Alabamas climbed to the surface on one side of the roots, and the Coushattas came out on the other side. Afterward they lived closely together but with a slightly different language.

Sunlight warmed the Earth's surface, plants and flowers grew in abundance, wildlife teemed in the forests and meadows. The people liked this different world. Yet they were not completely comfortable with such a vast change in their lives. They stayed outside at night, then returned to the cave when the sun rose in the east.

One night an owl hooted in the lofty reaches of the ancient tree as they explored the land nearby. Many of the people grew frightened and rushed back into the cave. They did not leave again. Yet others decided to live in the light of the new world. They stayed above ground and never returned to their former home.

If not for the hoot of the owl, more Alabama and Coushatta would walk the Earth today.

The Great Flood

One evening several of the people sat around a campfire, watching the flickering light of fireflies in the darkness. They relaxed after a long day's work.

Frog hopped up to them. "Beware. A great flood will cover the land with water."

They knew that could never happen so they laughed at Frog's joke.

"Beware," Frog croaked again. "A great flood will—"

Irritated, a man tossed Frog into the fire.

"Help!" Frog croaked.

Medicine Man pulled Frog out of the fire and took Frog home to nurse and heal the injured creature.

Soon Frog felt better. "Beware," Frog croaked. "A great flood will cover the land with water."

Three times Frog gave the warning, so Medicine Man believed the prediction. He grew afraid for his family and his people.

"What can we do?" he asked.

"You must build a raft with strong logs, then tie grass on the bottom to keep Beaver from cutting through the wood," Frog said.

Medicine Man hurried to his family with the news. His wife, his children, his wife's parents and grandparents all helped build the raft as strong as they could make it.

Frog looked the raft over and was satisfied.

They warned the rest of the village, but everyone laughed at Frog's joke and at the family who believed the prediction.

Soon the rains came, harder and harder. Swollen streams churned up lots of fish, and the people quickly caught them. They ate as they watched the rain, pleased to get such easy food.

"Beware," Frog croaked one final time. "A great flood will cover the land with water."

As the people laughed, Frog led the family along with many animals and birds to the raft. They got onboard and waited. Soon the water rose high, then higher. As they floated away, the people's laughter died away to silence.

Safe on the raft, they watched treetops, then mountaintops disappear beneath swirling water. The Winged Ones flew up and caught hold of the sky with their talons, but the tips of their tails became wet.

One bird flew so high the sun singed head feathers bright red, earning it the name Redheaded Woodpecker. Another bird's tail split in the rising water and became known as Scissor-Tail.

When Bear Lost Fire

Bear roamed through thick forests, eating sweet honey from beehives, fishing in rushing streams, and sleeping through long winters in deep, warm caves. Strong and powerful, Bear owned Fire.

Bear carried Fire everywhere, but one day Bear grew distracted by an abundance of tasty acorns. Bear set Fire on the ground, then gobbled up acorns with no thought to Fire.

Soon Fire burned low and grew afraid, for Bear moved farther away under ancient trees, tossing acorns into massive jaws.

"Help me!" Fire tried to burn brighter but with no success.

Bear didn't hear, having spotted a beehive. Thoughts of a thick yellow comb dripping with sticky sweetness danced in Bear's head.

"Feed me!" Fire called desperately, almost extinguished from lack of fuel.

The people gathered pecans under nearby trees. They heard Fire cry out, but they knew it was dangerous to go near Bear who owned Fire. Still they could not ignore the helpless cries.

"What do you eat?" the people asked.

"Wood. I need wood."

The people quickly gathered a piece of wood from each direction, then returned. They laid a stick across Fire toward the north. They laid a stick across Fire toward the west. They laid a stick across Fire toward the south. They laid a stick across Fire toward the east. And finally Fire blazed up.

"You saved me." Fire burned brightly.

A loud roar came from under the oak trees, and Bear rushed into the clearing. The people scattered in all directions, dropping their baskets of pecans.

Bear reached down to take back Fire but jerked away, burned for the first time.

"Go away," Fire said. "You forgot me so I no longer know you."

Bear rose up high on two legs, growling and whining, but to no avail. Fire no longer knew Bear, so the mighty beast lumbered unhappily away with no interest in acorns or honey now.

"Come get me," Fire called to the people. "If you take care of me, I will take care of you."

And the People came for Fire.

Illness Comes to the World

Medicine Man knew he would soon walk the spirit trail due to his advanced age. Death stalked him. He looked forward to joining his ancestors, but he worried about the people left without his medicine wisdom.

One day Soul Bieche, Giver-and-Taker-Away-of-the-Breath-of-Life, breathed words into his ear. "A messenger will arrive to tell you how to leave your medicine wisdom with your people before you set out on the spirit trail."

Medicine Man felt great relief at this news, and he slept better than he had in many nights.

Three days later, Soul Bieche breathed into his ear again. "I send a messenger to meet you under the lightning-split pecan tree at the edge of the forest."

Overjoyed at the news, Medicine Man tried to rise from his bed, but he was too weak to get up. He called for his two strong grandsons, and they hurried to his side.

"My legs no longer will carry me. You must go in my place to the lightning-split pecan tree at the edge of the forest. A messenger from Soul Bieche brings me word and you must get it for me."

"We will do so," one said.

"And soon return," the other added.

The young men set off at once, anxious to prove

themselves worthy of the great task. They knew the location of the tree and walked right to it. They looked around but saw nothing unusual, so they sat down to wait for the messenger.

Soon Rattlesnake slithered up beside them, raised his large head, and stared at them.

Frightened, they grabbed clubs and beat Rattlesnake to death. They hung his long, limp body over a branch of the pecan tree.

They saw no other danger so they sat back down to await Soul Bieche's messenger. They waited, watching the sun ride across the sky from the east to the west. Finally they gave up and returned to the village, their heads hung in defeat. They entered their home and went to Medicine Man's side.

"No messenger came," one said.

"But we killed a giant rattlesnake, the other added.

Medicine Man cried out in horror. "You killed the messenger. Now Soul Bieche is angry and trouble will come to our people." Medicine Man breathed his last breath after his prophecy, then he stepped onto the spirit trail.

Frightened, the young men ran back to the forest, making up a plan to save themselves.

They picked up Rattlesnake and carried him to their village. They placed him in front of an enemy's home, then hurried to a hiding place. The enemy found Rattlesnake, realized the danger, and put him in front of another home. As soon as Rattlesnake was discovered, he was placed in front of someone else's home. Everyone believed evil would come to them if Rattlesnake stayed in front of their home, so they kept moving him.

That night Rattlesnake's mate slithered into the

village. She was full of anger and determined on revenge. She laid an egg before every home where Rattlesnake had lain dead, then she carried his body back to their forest lair.

As the sun rose in the east, an illness hatched from each rattlesnake egg so that sickness entered the world.

Rescue of the Sun

An elder placed Sun in an earthen pot. She kept Sun there. Rabbit wanted Sun and danced into the village. Well-known as a trickster and a dancer, Rabbit gathered the people in front of Sun-Keeper's home.

"I will dance. Sing for me," Rabbit said.

"What is your song?" the people asked.

"Sing Rabbit, Rabbit, Rabbit."

"Rabbit, Rabbit, Rabbit," they sang.

Rabbit danced, powerfully as only Rabbit can dance.

"Move Sun closer to me."

They sang as they moved the pot forward.

"Closer still." Rabbit danced harder and faster.

They moved the pot forward again.

Rabbit grabbed Sun, then ran into the forest. The people chased, but Rabbit quickly outdistanced them.

As Rabbit ran, the pot banged against bushes, but it did not break. Finally Rabbit struck the pot on a horn-beam tree, it broke apart, and Sun spilled out.

From all over the forest creatures rushed to Sun. They called a great council to figure out how to put Sun back in the sky.

Flapping wings hard, Wren managed to get Sun up a short distance before Sun fell back again.

"If someone helps me, we can carry Sun up into the sky," Wren said.

Many of the other birds feared to fly that high, but Buzzard put one eye and then the other eye on Sun. "I believe we can do it."

Together, Wren and Buzzard grasped Sun on each side, flew up high, then higher yet, and placed Sun back in the sky. They returned to Earth in triumph.

Everyone agreed they deserved a reward.

"Buzzard, from now on you will eat dead animals and be immune to disease," the council said.

"And Wren, you will bathe in cold water each morning so you never get sick."

A Game of Water

Water Keeper played thlakalu'nka, the moccasin game. He sat on one side of a furry bearskin while his opponents sat on the other side. Four square pieces of deerskin lay on the bearskin. One player rolled a pebble around in two hands. After a while, he pretended to hide it to confuse the others before slipping it under one of the deerskins.

Water Keeper needed to guess where the pebble was hidden, or he would lose his turn. If he missed three times, one of his friends would try his luck so they could win the pebble. So far luck had failed him. As he grew more frustrated, he became reckless.

He bet what he owned and lost it all. His friends tried to stop him, but he started to bet other items. Soon he had nothing left except one. As Guardian-of-All-the-Water-of-the-World, he bet it. Again he lost.

All the water of the world, rivers, lakes, ponds, and other water, dried up.

Water Keeper felt bad about his actions, but he did not know how to bring back the water. The land grew parched. The people and animals hunted water everywhere. All would die if water was not found soon.

After four days Woodpecker heard water, and he flew to a cane the size of a tree. Perching on the cane, Woodpecker started to peck. A frightening noise came from inside, so Woodpecker flew away.

As the land grew more parched, Woodpecker became courageous and flew back to the cane. After several mighty pecks, water flowed out of the cane and filled all the lakes, streams, and ponds.

The people and animals rejoiced, drinking their fill of water.

Pigeon Hawk's Gift

A poor orphan boy hunted with the best bow and arrows he could get, but he had little success. No one in his village liked him because he brought nothing home from the hunt.

One day Orphan crossed a great river in search of game. He stayed with people who suggested he hunt in their area. With a pack on his back, he set out with bow and arrows. He reached a big thicket by nightfall. Discouraged because he had seen nothing to hunt all day, he sat under a tree.

"I may as well give up," he said. "I will never be a good hunter."

He built a campfire, sat down, and crossed his legs. As he watched the flames, he heard a noise.

Pigeon Hawk flew down and perched between his knees.

Horned Owl followed in close pursuit and landed on the other side of the fire.

"Hold me," Pigeon Hawk said.

Orphan set Pigeon Hawk on his knee.

"Toss Pigeon Hawk to me. I am hungry," Horned Owl said.

"Do not do that," Pigeon Hawk said.

"Throw me Pigeon Hawk," Horned Owl said. "And you will gain my power to kill."

"No," Pigeon Hawk said. "My way is better."

Orphan listened to the birds try to win him to their side, and he knew this might be his one chance to become a great hunter. Yet he did not know which bird to choose.

"Horned Owl is a powerful night shaman," Pigeon Hawk said. "Do not listen to him and I will give you good hunting in the morning."

"I can kill nothing," Orphan said. "I want to be a great hunter."

"Listen to me and you will be," Pigeon Hawk said.

"No. I am the better hunter," Horned Owl said. "Do as I say."

Orphan sat still all night long.

At dawn Horned Owl hooted, then flew to the top of a tree.

"Now let me go," Pigeon Hawk said.

Orphan released the bird.

Pigeon Hawk cried out before flying high into the sky to turn and dive at Horned Owl. One slash of Pigeon Hawk's sharp beak and Horned Owl fell dead to the ground.

"By day I am the best hunter." Pigeon Hawk flew back to Orphan. "Ask me for anything."

"I ask to be a great hunter."

Orphan picked up his bow and arrows and set out to hunt. Soon he killed bear, deer, turkey, and other game. He brought them back to his camp, cooked them, and felt happy. He no longer had to hunt far, for his keen eyes saw everything.

In time he went home to his village to share his hunting skills with them. But they still did not like him, because now he had too much success.

Corn Woman

Corn Woman walked long and far in search of her children. She could not find them, but she continued to look. In time dirt and sores covered her body, for she no longer cared about herself. Wherever she went, people shunned her

After a time she found orphan children who lived

alone. They needed a mother to care for them.

"Stay with us," they said.

"I will do that." She looked around their home. "Set out your cookware."

They set out pots.

She rubbed her body as she would rub corn-on-the-cob. Corn fell from her into the pots because she was Corn Woman. She made bread from the corn, and they ate their fill.

After a time her sores healed and she no longer went dirty. The orphans grew strong.

One day she examined the corn. "It grows hard." She checked an old corncrib nearby.

The orphans watched her in wonder.

"Sweep this corncrib clean, then close it," she said. I am your mother. You may eat bread made from white corn. Now go to sleep."

They did exactly as she asked and were soon inside their lodge. Later that night they heard rapping in the corncrib, then silence once more.

Early the next morning they went to the corncrib and discovered it full of corn.

ᎥᏓᎣᎴᎠᎴ

Journey to the Sky

Four elders decided to search for the end of the world. They packed deerskin bags with food, then selected knives, bows, and arrows for protection from wild animals.

As the sun rose in the east the next morning, they set out. They walked westward with the sun, because the sun would be less hot in the west after using up much of its heat during its journey across the sky.

They drank water from rushing streams, ate food from their bags, and slept peacefully the first night. On the second day, they were hungry. They saw a turkey on a limb of an oak tree. One elder notched an arrow and let it fly. The turkey fell to the ground. They hurried forward, but they found only a dead mosquito under the arrow. Surprised, they shook their heads and continued westward through dense forest.

After several days a huge black bear charged out of the thick undergrowth and then changed into a black hairy caterpillar. Surprised again, they marveled at the sight, but they would not let anything slow them down.

Soon a large eagle swooped out of the sky to attack them. They fought back so fiercely that even the talons and beak of the mighty bird could not defeat them.

Finally they reached a prairie of tall grass that stretched far and wide. A mountain loomed in the distance. They pushed into the tall grass and walked for many days before they arrived at the mountain. Yet it was no mountain at all. Instead a small tortoise crawled across the prairie until it no longer barred their way. By now they felt little surprise at what might cross their path.

They walked into a dense forest, and they saw many rattlesnakes. They could not take a step without touching one, so they pulled bark from a slippery elm tree to make leggings. As they walked through the forest, the rattlesnakes attacked until the elm bark hung in shreds on their legs.

Soon they came to a wide river. They wondered how to get across, then they checked their bags for food. One threw a roasted bird in the water. They waited. Alligator swam to shore, but they did not want Alligator. They threw out another bird. Loggerhead Turtle snapped up the food, but they did not want Turtle either. They tossed another roasted bird in the water. Horned Snake, with one blue and one red horn, swam to shore and ate it.

They leaped on Horned Snake's back, but they were out of food. They had only a few bones left, so they threw a bone out into the water. Horned Snake swam toward the bone and ate it, then they threw another bone and Horned Snake continued to swim across the water following the bones. When they reached the final bone, they were still far from shore. One elder pitched hard, and the bone landed on the far shore. Horned Snake swam to it, and they climbed down, giving thanks to Horned Snake for the ride.

They grew older as their journey lengthened into years, but they continued on their mission. After a time they heard two objects crashing together in the distance. Puzzled, they walked through a dense forest, listening to the sound get louder every day.

Finally they arrived at a prairie and saw the sky falling to strike the earth. The battle never stopped as the sky repeatedly opened and shut.

"We stand at the end of the world," one elder said.

"I never doubted we would get here," another said.

"When the sky opens, we should run through to the other side. Surely another world awaits us there."

"A good idea."

"No. That is dangerous."

Soon three elders agreed to explore the new world, but

the fourth remained afraid.

When the sky went up again, the first elder ran under. "I am Panther."

The second came right behind. "I am Wildcat."

The third followed closely. "I am Wolf."

"Wait!" The last elder saw the others pass safely to the other side and decided to join them. But time had passed. The sky was coming back to earth. As the fourth ran through, saying nothing, the sky crashed down and crushed the last one.

Three elders leaped high and caught the sky as it went up, pulling them into the land of another world.

A woman of age lived alone by a river with a young boy to assist her. When she saw the three elders, she motioned to the boy to give them a dipper.

The first elder dipped water from the river and tossed it to the east. The second threw water to the south. The third tossed water to the west. The fourth was no longer with them, so the woman threw water to the north.

"You may go forward now, but do not touch any animal or person."

"We will be careful."

They crossed the river, then wandered through lush grass and dense forests where winged-ones, four-leggeds, and two-leggeds lived peacefully and happily together. No jealousy, hatred, or illness existed to mar the perfection of this world.

After a time one elder accidentally touched a horse, and it turned into a skeleton. Horrified, they grew careful about how they traveled. Yet later another elder touched a young girl, and she turned into a skeleton. Finally they understood that the spirits of those who once lived on Earth dwelt here.

They continued to explore the new world until they saw another woman of age. They were hungry. She cooked squashes and gave three to each elder. When those were eaten, three more squashes appeared.

She gave them many seeds for corn, sweet potato, bean, potato, and others, then they fell asleep.

When they awoke the next morning, they were in their own beds at home. With much celebration, they shared their adventures and seeds with the people.

Snake Woman

One day a woman carried buffalo grease in a pot as she left home. She walked beside her husband. When they reached the riverbank, she found some turtle eggs.

"These look good to eat," she said.

"Do not cook them in buffalo grease," he warned.

"I think that is the best way to cook them."

She built a small fire, then fried the eggs in the buffalo grease.

"Do not eat those eggs," he warned.

"They smell too good not to eat."

She sampled the eggs. "These are delicious." She took several bites until she ate them all.

As soon as she swallowed the last bite, her legs twisted until they resembled the tail of a snake.

"Stay away from the water," her husband warned.

She rolled toward the water. He tried to stop her, but she rolled too fast and splashed into the river. She disappeared into its depths.

"Come back," he called.

Other people rushed down to the riverbank. They wailed in despair and called her too.

After they called four times, she rose to the surface. She appeared completely as a snake. She looked at them all before turning back down into the water.

They never saw her again.

Terrapin Aids Opossum

In a warm and cozy nest lived Opossum with her many children. At night she had to go out to hunt for food, but she did not like to leave them alone.

One time Big Bat saw her leave, and he flew down, grabbed her babies, and carried them to a hole in the rocky side of a cliff.

She moaned in horror at the sight. She started after her children, crying aloud as she walked.

"What is wrong?" Wolf loped up to her.

"Big Bat stole my babies."

"Will you show me the place?"

"I am headed there now, but I do not know if I can help them."

"I will do what I can."

When they reached the bottom of the cliff, Opossum indicated the hollow in the rocks.

Wolf climbed swiftly upward and disappeared into the hollow. Almost immediately Wolf popped back out and ran away as if chased by a monster.

"I cannot do it." Wolf shook hard, then ran away.

Now Opossum felt even more terrified, because Wolf was known to be very brave. She started to cry again, fearing she would never get her children back.

"Why are you crying?" Rabbit hopped up.

"Big Bat stole my children."

"Where are they now?"

She indicated the hollow in the rock.

"I will get them for you."

Rabbit climbed the rocks, leaped into the hollow, then raced back out as if chased by a giant monster.

"What is wrong?"

"I can do nothing." Rabbit ran out of sight.

Now she felt a terrible agony, but she started up the cliff to save her babies. She cried as she went.

"Why do you cry?" Terrapin, a fresh water turtle, crawled up to her.

"Big Bat stole my babies."

"Where are they?"

"Up there in that hollow."

Terrapin disappeared into the hollow and crawled across hot ashes. "Ouch!" But that did not stop Terrapin, who grabbed the little opossums, then turned and hurried back outside.

"Here are your babies," Terrapin said.

"Thank you." Opossum looked up to see Big Bat fly out of the hollow and disappear.

"You must be more careful." Terrapin cut open the skin under Opossum's stomach. "Keep your babies here until they are old enough to go about by themselves."

"I will do that." She nestled her babies close before she started back toward their cozy nest.

Crane Challenges Hummingbird to a Race

"You are slow!" Hummingbird zipped round Crane several times, then hovered in front of Crane's beak.

"I am steady," Crane replied.

"You are heavy." Hummingbird flitted around Crane, pulled a tail feather, and then zipped back in front.

"Go poke a flower," Crane said, feeling irritated.

"How about a sharp beak to you." Hummingbird flashed fancy feathers in the sunlight.

"I could swallow you whole." Crane grew angry.

"Try to catch me if you can." Hummingbird zipped all around Crane, then hovered just out of range.

"I am faster than you."

"No, you are not."

"Yes, I am." Crane thought a moment. "I will prove it."

"How?" Hummingbird decided to play along with the joke.

"I propose a race to the ocean. The winner gets to live near water forever."

"Yes! A race." Hummingbird knew this would be an easy win and could already taste sweet victory.

They set the time and place to start. Hummingbird swept away in a flash of feathers, leaving Crane far behind. Hummingbird flew happily all day, made great progress, and perched in an ancient oak tree as the sun went down.

Crane flew through the sky all day and long into the night, passing Hummingbird overhead about midnight. Hummingbird heard the flap of Crane's wings and woke up. Grumpy from lack of sleep, Hummingbird took to the air and quickly flew far ahead of Crane.

Eager for a perch on the second night, Hummingbird selected a high branch on a tall birch tree and quickly went to sleep. Along about midnight the noise of Crane's flapping wings woke Hummingbird, who quickly took to the air and left Crane far behind.

Crane flew steadily all day and into the night, thinking about the situation. About midnight, Crane saw Hummingbird perched sound asleep in a pecan tree. Crane simply flew high into the sky to glide silently past overhead.

Hummingbird completed the race the next day only to discover Crane enjoying the ocean. To this day, Crane has the right to live near water.

Little-Yellow-Mouse Confronts Owl

One day Owl grew hungry, and so he flew to the home of Little-Yellow-Mouse for a feast. Owl sat down outside the front door and hooted.

Little-Yellow-Mouse peeked outside.

"What am I called when people hear me hoot at night?" Owl asked.

"Night Chief," Little-Yellow-Mouse said.

Owl hooted, pleased at the reply.

"What do they call me?" Owl asked again, preening feathers.

"Night Chief," Little-Yellow-Mouse said.

Owl repeated the question over and over, never tiring of the sound of Night Chief.

Finally Little-Yellow-Mouse grew angry. "Some people call you Big Eye."

"What?" Owl asked.

Little-Yellow-Mouse scurried away.

"No!" Owl hooted in fury. "I will forever be angry with you. Come here."

Little-Yellow-Mouse made not a single sound, hidden deep in a safe home.

Owl stayed at Little-Yellow-Mouse's front door until dead of hunger and thirst.

Tar Baby

One morning the people stood in their garden, shaking their heads at the destruction. During the night Rabbit had stolen watermelons, onions, and other vegetables again.

"How can we stop Rabbit?" someone asked.

"If one of us stood here all night long, Rabbit would be scared away."

"That will not do. We need our rest at night to work during the day."

"What about a tar baby?" another asked. "We could make an image in the shape of a man, leave it in the garden, and Rabbit would stay away."

They discussed the idea until everyone agreed it was a wise course of action. Soon they made the figure out of wood and grass, then they rubbed it with pine pitch to hold it together. They planted the tar baby in a standing position in the middle of the garden.

They stepped back, looked it over in satisfaction, and then walked home. They went to bed early that night.

While the people slept, Rabbit walked up to the edge of the garden. He stopped in surprise. A man stood in the middle of the vegetables. He stepped up close and stuck out his hand for a friendly shake, but he got no response.

"Oho. What have we here?" Rabbit slapped the man, but his paw stuck.

"This calls for another hand." Rabbit struck the man with his other hand, but it stuck too.

"Oho. This is curious. I can kick too." Rabbit kicked the man, but his foot stuck.

"My other foot will do." Rabbit kicked out with his foot, but it stuck too.

"Oho. This is a trick."

As the sun came up the next morning, the people hurried out to their garden. They saw Rabbit stuck to tar baby.

"Here is our thief," someone said.

"But not for long."

They grabbed Rabbit, freed him from the tar baby, and pushed him into a wooden box. They nailed it shut, then carried him to a nearby stream. They set the box down on the bank.

"That was hard work," someone said.

"Let us eat before we finish with Rabbit."

They made sure the box was secure, then walked away.

"Oho. I must get free." Rabbit set about wailing for help.

After a time a man from another tribe walked up. "Why do you cry?"

"They plan to send me to some pretty women, but I

do not want to go. I believe I will get hurt."

"I would like to go somewhere and see some pretty women," the man said. "I will go in your place."

"Oho. Let me out."

The man pried open the box. Rabbit stepped out, looked around to make sure nobody watched, then held up the lid as the man lay down inside.

"Be quiet and you will go." Rabbit nailed the lid shut and quickly walked away. From a distance he watched to see what the people would do.

After their meal they came back. They rolled the box into the water. Soon a current caught the box and carried it downstream.

Rabbit mulled over the incident, then he decided on a course of action. He went to a certain place. When he returned, he drove a herd of sheep up to the people's village.

They were surprised to see him, for they believed they had sent him to his death.

"I am here to thank you," Rabbit said. "That was the best trip I ever took."

"How so?" someone asked.

"Look at all these sheep I got in the place where you sent me. I wish you would nail me in a box and send me again."

"Could you get more sheep?"

"Oho. Not only that, many pretty women wanted me to stay. A man never wants to leave there." Rabbit looked around the group. "Are you ready to send me again?"

"No. Not you," one said. "I want to go."

"Are you sure?" Rabbit asked.

"Yes. And I will come back with sheep."

The people put him in a box and rolled it into the

stream.

Rabbit watched the box float away before he left to take care of other business. After a time he returned to the village.

"Our friend did not come back," someone said.

"I am not surprised," Rabbit said. "I told you that a man who went there would never want to return."

"He should not be the only one who gets to go," another said. "Let me."

Soon one man after another got into a box and floated down the stream.

Rabbit watched them go, then he left again. After a time he came back to see the people. He found them pulling a box out of the water. They opened the lid and saw one of their friends inside. Dead.

"Oho." Rabbit turned and ran.

The people chased him across the garden into the woods. Crane flew with them.

Rabbit leaped into a hollow tree and hid, but Crane found him. While the people went to get an ax to chop Rabbit out of the tree, Crane remained on guard.

After awhile Rabbit laughed inside the tree.

"What is funny?" Crane asked. "You are not in a position to laugh about anything."

Rabbit laughed harder.

"You should cry instead of laugh," Crane said. "Soon they will return with the ax and chop your heart out."

Rabbit laughed harder still.

"Stop that."

"Look here," Rabbit said.

"Where?"

"Inside the tree. You would not believe what is in here with me."

"What is in there?"

"You must look. I have no words to describe this amazing sight."

Crane peeked inside but jerked back out. "I saw nothing unusual."

"You did not look far enough inside."

Crane looked inside again, stretching a long neck.

Rabbit jerked a cord around Crane's neck and pulled hard until Crane fell over dead.

Rabbit leaped from the tree and ran away, but in the distance dogs bayed on his trail. At the sound, Rabbit knew fear, so he ran hard and fast.

Rabbit Tricks Wildcat

One day Rabbit traveled along, looking here and looking there. He saw a horse lying on the ground asleep in the shade of a pecan tree.

This looked of interest, so Rabbit sat down to watch. Nothing much happened, and he wondered what type of dreams ran through a horse's mind. He puzzled over this awhile, then he wondered how fast the horse would wake up if he hit the sensitive nose with pecans.

After a time Wildcat strolled up.

"Look what I killed."

"Big." Wildcat sniffed the air.

"Hungry?"

"Yes, I am."

"When I skin this animal, you may help me eat."

Wildcat sat down. "I will wait."

"I do not mind if you sit on my kill while I skin it. That way you can make sure I do it right."

"Are you sure?"

"Go ahead."

Wildcat walked over to the horse and leaped up on the broad back.

The horse's eyes snapped open and then it surged to its feet and started to buck.

Wildcat snarled. The horse reared up, came down hard on all four hooves, then raced away with Wildcat sticking to its back.

Little People

A race of little people exists for whom large is small and small is large.

One day a certain number of these people decided they would go to war. They made bows about six inches long and arrows even smaller. They set out on the warpath.

Soon a large person joined them, a shaman who had fasted four days to be able to see the little people.

They came upon a hive of yellow jackets, a sworn enemy of the little people. They fought hard, but the yellow jackets stung a good number of them to death. The large person jerked a bush out of the ground and beat the yellow jackets until they lay dead.

The little people greatly appreciated this help, so they

honored the large person with much affection.

They continued on their way and came to a small creek, but it was so big to the little people that they built rafts to cross.

Soon they killed *tsishtsinuk,* a small bird, and cut it into pieces to carry separately because it was so heavy. When the large person lifted the bird's head by the bill, they saw amazing strength.

When they came to a small creek, the large person would put them in a big hand and set them on the other side. Yet when they came to a big creek, they could jump over but they had to help the large person across.

They killed a buffalo, and a little person picked up the mighty beast to carry alone.

Finally they came to a place where many cranes lived along the water. They fought hard, but the cranes killed many little people. The large person clubbed the cranes until they flew away, then they continued on the warpath.

Old Dog

One day a man picked up his bow and his quiver of arrows, then stepped outside his home.

He patted Old Dog on the head. "You stay here and watch the house."

Old Dog whined and wagged a tail.

Starting down the trail, he looked about at the beautiful day, then he realized Old Dog followed him.

"No. You stay home."

Old Dog whined and wagged a tail.

He started back down the trail, but Old Dog followed. He stopped again.

Old Dog whined and wagged a tail.

"I do not know why you are following me. Go home."

He walked deep into the woods, then sat down on a fallen log and made a fire.

Old Dog loped into camp, sat down, and whined.

"Why are you here? Why do you whine?"

"I whine because I am sorry for you," Old Dog said. "People follow who want to kill you."

He looked back down the trail in concern. "Are you sure?"

"Yes. I waited and watched."

"They must not catch me."

"They are too close to escape." Old Dog glanced around the camp. "You need to fool them. Gather a lot of wood, put it on the ground near the fire, and cover it with a blanket so it looks like a man asleep."

He got up to follow Old Dog's instructions.

"When they see the blanket, they will think it is you and shoot the blanket."

He piled wood in place.

"You hide in the trees and watch. When they bend over to see if you are dead, you shoot one. The other will escape. You run after him and kill him with your knife."

He laid a blanket over the wood.

"When you get home, feed me first."

He hid in the bushes, then watched Old Dog leave camp toward home.

Soon the two men walked into camp, shot the blanket, then bent over it. He shot one, stabbed the other, then broke camp.

When he reached home, Old Dog waited for him.

"Thank you. You saved my life." He fixed the best meal he ever had for Old Dog.

Old Dog ate the food and then walked to the edge of the yard. A glance back, a long howl, then Old Dog laid down and died.

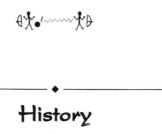

History

Across the Southeastern Woodlands stretching from the Carolinas to East Texas, the Mississippian culture grew out of a land of ancient forests and rushing streams. For thousands of years, the gentle climate and abundant land nurtured the people who created complex cultures that built flat-topped, earthen pyramids for ceremonial centers.

The Alabama and Coushatta were part of the powerful League of the Muskogulgee, or Upper Creek Confederacy, with a Muskhogean language.

From the Muskogee migration legend, the Atilamas, or Alabama, and three other ancient tribes migrated from the West to settle east of the Mississippi River.

Alabama, sometimes Alabamu, from the Choctaw *alba'lmo*, means "medicine gatherers" or "thicket clearers." Coushatta, or Kosati, from the Choctaw *kanshak* and *hata*, means "white cane." Cane knives used by Southeastern tribes were called *kanshak*.

The Alabama and Coushatta lived near each other in a land blessed by Soul Bieche, the Giver and Taker Away of the Breath of Life. They revered the Earth, for their mythic tradition stated that Soul Bieche caused them to spring from the rich soil of their ancestral land.

In this fertile country, men and women worked together in agriculture, growing large crops of corn and other vegetables in fenced fields outside their communities. They hunted, fished, and gathered fruit, berries, nuts, and herbs.

In textiles, they wove cloth from a variety of fibers such as opossum hair and buffalo wool. In the decorative arts, they excelled with ceremonial robes of brilliant feathers and copper ornaments and beadwork accented with a scroll design based on their ancient Sun worship. Their unique baskets and pottery were highly prized throughout their extensive trade network.

In personal appearance, the women stood about five feet tall with the men slightly taller. They bathed every day, no matter the weather, as a spiritual and physical cleansing. They wore a copper nose ring and earrings of copper, beads, colored stones, or bones. Necklaces made of strings of beads or pearls were worn around the neck. They also painted their bodies, preferring red, black, and yellow colors, and sometimes added a tattoo.

Men wore deerskin breechclouts and belts of skin strung with beads. In winter they added deerskin mantles and skin leggings. Usually they went barefoot, but if needed they wore Southeastern swamp moccasins. They might add a feather robe for ceremony or high status. They styled their hair in a roach or in braids, two in front and two in back.

Women wore an apron skirt woven of bark or nettle and a shawl or cape covered one breast only, leaving the right arm free. For travel or winter, they might add knee-high leggings and a mantle of bear, deer, panther, buffalo, beaver, or other fur. They wore their hair parted in the middle and pulled back into a large bun and fastened with a bone hairpin and tied with a cord.

The Alabama and Coushatta brought their creative spirit to the construction of their villages. Homes radiated outward from a central public square used for councils, ceremonies, and games. Here they built a temple, a council house, and other buildings to house their sacred tribal possessions such as the peace pipe, drums, or articles used by medicine makers and prophets.

A family home site usually consisted of four round houses built in a square, containing a kitchen and winter lodging house, a visitor hall and summer lodging house, a granary, and a warehouse. The yards were cleared of grass, for they believed that this precaution kept sickness away. All homes belonged to the women.

With a culture based on a matriarchal clan system, all recognized family descent came through the woman's line. A man married into a woman's clan, and he lived with her family. She stayed near her clan or lived in her mother's home with her husband and children. A man and his clan had no legal rights in the children's family concerns, and primarily women trained children. Clan children were educated by elders in the ways of their culture. The chieftainship descended strictly through the female line.

To be a member of a clan meant citizenship in the tribe with social, political, and religious privileges. The principal clan councils of the Alabama were the Deer, Bear, Beaver, Alligator, Panther, Turkey, Wolf, Daddy-Long-Legs, Wind, and Salt. The Coushatta belonged to the Bear, Raccoon, Alligator, Beaver, Bird, Panther, Wildcat, Deer, Daddy-Long-Legs, and Wind clans. Men and women never married within the same clan.

The clans were divided into opposite fires, with the White Clans maintaining peace and the Red Clans waging war. They lived in separate villages and avoided each other, except for special functions of war and peace and ball games.

Religion played a vital role in their lives. The Green Corn Ceremony may be one of the oldest unbroken ceremonial traditions in America. A series of four rituals, three stamp dances set to song, drum, rattle, and flute, culminated in the Busk. From *buskita*, to fast, the Busk was held when the green corn ripened. The people ritually cleansed their bodies to eat the new corn. All fires were extinguished, then a new Sacred Fire was built. Violations committed during the year were forgiven, and all was restored for the new year. At the end of the Busk, the women carried a flame from the new Sacred Fire to start the central fire in their homes.

An elected *miko*, or chief, handled civil affairs, particularly the council house and the public granary. An assistant chief helped the *miko* to receive visitors, make public addresses, and confer with the council and other advisors on important matters.

Warriors went to the council house for four days before they started on the warpath. A medicine man led them in war songs and gave them war medicine to drink. When the war captain beat a drum three times around his winter house, the warriors gathered their weapons and provisions. The war captain carried the war bundle, or Sacred Ark, that would allow them to defeat their enemies. They gave war whoops as they marched out of the village to fight naked against their enemies, for apparel fragments made a wound more dangerous than a clean wound.

After battle they made peace with as much solemn ritual as they made war. Enemies ate together and smoked the peace pipe. Painted white for peace, the warriors danced and sang a sacred song, calling for Soul Bieche to witness their goodwill.

In 1541 Hernando de Soto brought Spanish soldiers to the Southeast. He came to steal the treasures of *El Dorado*, a fabled land of great riches. They wore steel helmets and breastplates, and they carried shields, swords, and crossbows. They brought cannon, horses, mules, cattle, hogs, skilled workers with equipment to refine gold, and two years' worth of provisions. Packed in trunks and ready for use were handcuffs, chains, and neck collars to make slaves of resistive natives.

De Soto made contact with the Alabama in northern Mississippi and the Coushatta on Pine Island in the Tennessee River, or River of the Cussatees.

The Spaniards were more interested in gold than in hospitality, so they cut a swath of death and destruction across the Southeast. They never found *El Dorado* because it did not exist. At the Father of Waters, De Soto sickened and died. The Spaniards buried him in the Mississippi River, then continued their path of destruction into East Texas.

As soldiers and settlers from England, France, and Spain pushed into their new world, they brought European diseases such as smallpox. Their diseases ran far ahead of actual contact with the Indians. With no natural immunity or effective medicine, epidemics quickly killed up to ninety-five percent of the inhabitants of villages. Those who lived migrated to band together for survival and protection, and they saved fragments of their cultures.

By 1684 a part of the Coushatta lived on the right bank of the Alabama River, three miles below the fork of the Coosa and Tallapoosa. Alabamas also migrated to settle near the Coushattas. Their villages stretched for forty miles on both sides of the Alabama River. Later two more large villages of Coushattas settled in the area. They strengthened the Creek Confederacy, and all participated in Creek tribal ceremonies.

When the French arrived to establish settlements at Mobile, the Alabama, a red war tribe, fought them along with the Mobile. After a time they established peace, and the Alabamas developed a loyalty to French traders that concerned the English in the area.

In 1714 Fort Toulouse was constructed deep in the Alabama and Coushatta homeland. The fort provided protection, but it was also their trading center. Animal skins and other natural products were floated down the Alabama River to Mobile at the Gulf of Mexico while European products were carried upriver.

After the French lost the French and Indian War in 1763, they relinquished Fort Toulouse to the English. Soon new officials and settlers arrived. The European market for skins was inexhaustible, but the number of animals, even in an area once teeming with wildlife, was limited. The Southeast was now overhunted, and the tribes were fighting each other over hunting land because they had become dependent on European products.

Anglo-American settlers were pressing inland from the Atlantic coast.

Alabamas and Coushattas began to follow their French allies to Louisiana. By 1766 a few Alabamas were already settled on the Sabine River. More followed. In 1780 Alabamas and Coushattas crossed the Sabine River and settled on the Trinity River in Texas. They were invited by the Spanish who wanted an outer guard against the French and after 1803, the Americans.

They moved deep into the Big Thicket where they found safety in an abundant wilderness. They began new lives. They built villages of log cabins, then connected them with a network of trails through dense forest. They hunted, fished, and traded with the Caddo, the French, and Anglo-American settlers. They raised cattle, horses, and hogs. They grew corn, potatoes, beans, yams, and picked fruit and berries. Although still plagued by epidemics, they adapted to a new culture.

By the nineteenth century they wore Anglo-American clothes. The women dressed in calico skirts and blouses with wool shawls for warmth. The men adopted full-skirted coats, cotton shirts, cravats, and trousers. They wore shoes.

In Alabama, a large number of Alabamas and Coushattas remained at Kanchati, Red Ground, in their homeland. In 1813-14 the Alabama were considered among the fiercest warriors in the Creek War. After their defeat by the United States army, they were forced to move north of their old villages. In 1836 the United States removed them along with the Creek to Indian Territory. Afterward they were counted as part of Creek Nation, West.

In Texas, the Coahuila and Texas commissioner

surveyed the native population in 1831. A report stated that 600 Alabamas lived in three villages on the Neches and 400 Coushatta lived in two villages on the Trinity. The Spanish Crown and later the Republic of Mexico kept the borderlands around the two tribes unsettled to protect them from Anglo-American settlers.

The Alabama and Coushatta prospered in peace until Texas won its independence from Mexico in 1836. Although they remained neutral, even helped Anglo-Texans in their fight for independence by providing a safe haven for refugees, they were soon included in the new republic's policy of removal, reservation, or extermination for all Indians within its borders.

Alabama and Coushatta land and villages were claimed by Anglo-Americans who poured into the area to farm and ranch. Alabamas drifted in one direction and the Coushattas in another as they searched the Big Thicket for a place to live in peace.

In 1845 the Republic of Texas became the State of Texas, and the United States requested that land be set aside for reservations. The Alabama and Coushatta petitioned for reserve land. The Texas legislature refused but finally relented after years of fighting with the Plains Indians.

The Alabama received a 1,100.7-acre reservation in Polk County in 1854. The Texas legislature appropriated funds in 1855 for a 640-acre reserve for the Coushatta, but no land in East Texas could be found for them. At the same time two reservations were established on the Brazos River for the other Indians in Texas.

In 1858 the State of Texas wanted to move Alabamas and Coushattas to the Brazos Reserve. Not long after, Anglo-Texans killed Caddos there, and the Alabama and

Coushatta agent decided they would not be safe on the Brazos Reserve, so they were allowed to remain in East Texas. In 1859 the Coushattas settled on the Alabama reservation.

During the War Between the States, the Alabama and Coushatta served the Confederate States of America by transporting East Texas produce from plantations on flat-bottom riverboats to the Gulf Coast.

After the war they had reservation land, but times grew harder. Anglo-American settlers pushed into Texas with little respect for the reserve's boundaries. Loggers rapidly felled the forests. Plowing land under for farms almost destroyed the hunting, fishing, and gathering economy. They lost reservation land to a railroad grant. Hunger and disease caused a sharp population decline.

Finally, in 1880, the Alabama and Coushatta started a slow road to recovery, but it was at the expense of their own heritage. A railroad line was built into the Big Thicket, allowing a lumber industry to develop. For the first time, they learned to work for wages. A Presbyterian mission and school were established to teach a new language, religion, and culture. A local attorney started a long campaign to get help from state and federal governments.

The people adapted to the Anglo-American culture to survive. Their spiritual belief and expression remained strong even though the acceptance of Christianity greatly modified their religion. They also gave up another tradition vital to their heritage as individual desire took precedence over the well-being of the community. Despite these drastic changes, women retained significant roles as tribal leaders and clan elders as they had in their matriarchy.

In 1924 the Alabama and Coushatta, along with other Indians, became United States citizens. In 1928 federal funds provided relief with the purchase of 3,071 acres of additional reservation land. In 1941 many tribal members joined the United States armed forces and served heroically in World War II. In 1948 the Texas attorney general confirmed their voting rights.

In 1962 they established the Tribal Enterprise Tourist Project. In 1989 the Chief Kina Medical Center was dedicated. And in 1994 work began on the Alabama-Coushatta Cultural Center.

At 4,600 acres, the Alabama-Coushatta Indian Reservation deep in the Big Thicket near Lake Livingston is the largest and oldest in the state of Texas. After five hundred years of cultural transition, Alabamas and Coushattas still practice elements of their traditional religion and medicine, and their language is being taught again.

Tribal Enterprises of the Alabama-Coushatta Tribe of Texas offers a wide variety of opportunities to experience traditional Indian culture. Tribal dances, back country trips, nature walks, a historical museum, arts and crafts, campgrounds, and the Indian Chief train draw many people to visit the Alabama-Coushatta.

Sources

Caddo Confederacies

Dorsey, George A. *Traditions of the Caddo.* Publication Number 41. "The Origin of Animals," p. 14. "The Second Man Who Came Out of the Earth," pp. 17-18, as told by White-Bread. "Evening-Star and Orphan-Star," pp. 26-27. "The Girl who Married a Star," pp. 29-30, as told by Annie Wilson. "The Orphan Boy Who Became a Wrestler," pp. 45-46, as told by Wing. "The Girl Who Had Power to Call the Buffalo," pp. 51-52. "The Old Woman Who Kept All the Pecans," p. 52, as told by Wing. "The Power of the Cyclone," p. 56, as told by Wing. "The Young Men and the Cannibals," pp. 58-59, as told by Wing. "The Death of the Cannibals," pp. 61-62, as told by Shorter. "The Man Who Made Arrows for Ghost," pp. 63-64, as told by Wing. "The Turtle Who Carried the People Away," p. 81, as told by Wing. "Why Hawks Have Thin Legs," p. 83, as told by White-Bread. "How Rabbit Stole Mountain-Lion's Teeth," pp. 85-86, as told by Wing. "Coyote, Mountain-Lion, and Rabbit," p. 100, as told by Wing. "Coyote Turns into a Corn Mill," p. 108, as told by Wing. Washington D.C.: Carnegie Institution of Washington, 1905. Lincoln: University of Nebraska Press, 1997.

George A. Dorsey, Carnegie Institution of Washington, collected these tales from 1903-1905 from the Caddo living in western Oklahoma. His primary sources were Wing, Annie Wilson, White House (Caddo Jack), White-Bread, Caddo George, Shorter, Hinie, and Moon-Light.

Lipan Apache

Opler, Morris Edward. *Myths and Legends of the Lipan Apache Indians.* "The Emergence," pp. 13-16. "The Birth of Killer-of-Enemies," pp. 16-22. "Killer-of-Enemies and His Brother, Wise One, Slay More Monsters," pp. 22-26. "Killer-of-Enemies Teaches Raiding and Warfare and Departs," pp. 36-37. "The Woman Saved by the Prairie-Dogs," pp. 72-74. "The Man Who Knew a Horse Ceremony Obtains Horses," pp. 78-79. "How Rabbit Stole Mountain-Lion's Teeth," pp. 85-86. "The Quarrel Between Wind and Thunder," p. 86. "The Girl Who Was Rescued by her Dead Father," pp. 101-104. "Coyote Gets the Buffaloes Away from Crow," pp. 122-125. "Coyote and Wildcat Scratch Each Other's Backs," pp. 191-192. "The Fearless Man: The Adventure with the Snakes," pp. 275-277. "The Woman who Acted Like a Deer," p. 285. New York: J. J. Augustin Publisher, 1940.

Morris Edward Opler collected these myths and legends in 1935 on the Mescalero Apache reservation in New Mexico from Antonio Apache, Stella La Paz, and Percy Bigmouth. All myths retold here are from Antonio Apache except for "Coyote and Wildcat Scratch Each Other Backs" from Percy Bigmouth.

Wichita Confederacy

Dorsey, George A. *The Mythology of the Wichita*. "The Thunderbird-Woman," pp. 120-123, as told by Ahahe (Waco). "The Hawk and His Four Dogs," pp. 129-130, as told by Towakoni Jim (Towakoni). "The Spiders Who Recovered the Chief's Grandson," pp. 177-187, as told by Ahahe (Waco). "The Story of Not-Know-Who-You-Are," pp. 224-228, as told by Ahahe (Waco). "The Turtle's War-Party," pp. 242-243, as told by Ahahe (Waco). "The Boy who Led War-Parties and Became a Hawk," pp. 257-263, as told by Cheater (Wichita). "The Coyote and the Skunk, who Inaugurated the Feast," pp. 276-278, as told by Towakoni Jim (Towakoni). "The Coyote and the Smallest Snake," p. 289, as told by Ignorant Woman (Towakoni). John, Elizabeth A. H., "Foreword," 1995. Washington D.C.: Carnegie Institution, 1904. Norman: University of Oklahoma Press, 1995.

George A. Dorsey, under a grant from the Carnegie Institution of Washington, collected these myths from 1900 to 1903 in Oklahoma. Wichita Burgess Hunt interpreted, and Wichita Chief Towakoni Jim gave invaluable assistance.

Comanche

Barnard, Herwanna Becker. *The Comanche and His Literature with an Anthology of His Myths, Legends, Folktales, Oratory, Poetry, and Songs* "Origin of Days and Seasons," as told in 1940 by Rachel Mow-wat as she heard it from her father-in-law, Mow-wat, pp. 79-80. "How the Spots on the Moon Originated," as told in 1940 by Tehquakuh through interpreter, Herman Asenap, pp. 88-93. "The Deer That Ate People," as told by Rachel Mow-wat in July 1940, pp. 99-100. "Two Buffaloes That Spoke," as told by Tehquakuh through interpreter Herman Asenap in July 1940, pp. 101-102. "Netah's Sacrifice" by Randlett Parker, pp. 108-109. "What Became of the Great Giant," as told by Mow-wat and interrupted by Rachel Mow-wat in June 1940, p. 121. "The Comanche Boy Who Was Captured," as told by Rachel Mow-wat in July 1940, pp. 123-125. "Nu'ah Nuh," as told by Rachel Mow-wat in July 1940, pp. 126-127. "A Raid for Horses," as told by Felix Koweno in June 1940, pp. 139-140. "Eh'Kap-Tuh'" as told in 1940 by Rachel Mow-wat, pp. 186-187. "The Otter and the Fox," as told by Mow-wat and interpreted by Rachel Mow-wat, pp. 229-230. "How Fox Became Blind," as told by Mow-wat and translated by Rachel Mow-wat, pp. 231-232. "The Race Between Rabbit and Turtle," pp. 244-246. "The Coyote Girl" as told in 1940 by Herman Asenap as he heard it from Tehquahkuh, pp. 250-252. Graduate thesis. Norman: The University of Oklahoma, 1941.

Herwanna Becker Baker collected these stories in Oklahoma.

St. Clair, H. H. and Lowie, R. H. *Journal of American Folklore*, XXII. "Shoshone and Comanche Tales: The Deserted Children," pp. 275-276. Also, Becker, 94-97.

Reid, Mrs. Bruce. *Legends of Texas*. "An Indian Legend of the Blue Bonnet," pp. 197-200. Dobie, J. Frank, ed. Also Becker, pp. 110-114. Austin: Texas Folklore Society, 1924.

"She Who Is Alone's Sacrifice." Comanche Lodge Web Site Online 1999.

Alabama and Coushatta

Lankford, George E. *Native American Legends: Southeastern Legends: Tales from the Natchez, Caddo, Biloxi, Chickasaw, and Other Nations.* "Bears and Fire," pp. 69-70. Emergence," p. 111. "The Flood," pp. 110-111. "The Rescue of the Sun," p. 66. "The Impounded Water," pp. 128-129. "The Marooned Hero," pp. 206-208. "Journey to the Sky," pp. 211-121. Little Rock: August House, 1987.

George E. Lankford's primary sources are from documented material.

Martin, Howard N. *Myths and Legends of the Alabama-Coushatta Indians of Texas.* "Origin of the Alabama and Coushatta Tribes," p. 3. "How the Sun Came to the Sky," p. 6. "How Water Was Lost and Found," p. 7. "How Fire Came to the Alabamas and Coushattas," p. 8. "The Great Flood," pp. 9-10. "A Race Between Crane and Hummingbird," p. 18. "A Journey to the Sky," pp. 24-27. Austin: The Encino Press, 1977.

Howard N. Martin collected these myths and legends between 1931 and 1940 from nineteen Alabama-Coushatta storytellers on their reservation near his hometown of Livingston, Texas. Primary sources were Charles Martin Thompson, or Sun-Ke, McConico Battise, Bronson Cooper Sylestine, Charles Boatman, Billy Harrison Battise, Frank Sylestine, and Gustin Battise, as well as folklore collectors James L. D. Sylestine, Matthew Bullock, and Clem Fain Jr.

Rothe, Aline. *Kalita's People: A History of the Alabama-Coushatta Indians of Texas*, pp. 13, 21-22. Waco, Texas: Texian Press, 1963.

Swanton, John R. *Myths and Tales of the Southeastern Indians.*
"The Flood" (Alabama), p. 121. "Fire" (Alabama), p. 122.
"The Rescue of the Sun" (Alabama), p. 123. "How Water
was Lost and Recovered" (Alabama), pp. 123-124. "The
Men Who Went to the Sky" (Alabama), pp. 139-143.
"The Woman Who Turned into a Snake" (Alabama), p.
154. "Crane and Humming Bird Race" (Alabama), p.
157. "Corn Woman" (Koasati), p. 168. "How the Water
Was Lost and Recovered" (Koasati), p. 168. "The Old
Dog Saves His Master" (Koasati), p. 194. "The Pigeon
Hawk's Gift" (Koasati), pp. 194-195. "The Story of Owl
and Little Yellow Mouse" (Koasati), p. 198. "The Story of
Opossum" (Koasati), pp. 199-200. "Crane and Humming-
bird" (Koasati), pp. 201-202. "The Tar Baby" (Koasati),
pp. 208-209. "Rabbit Fools Wildcat" (Koasati), p. 211.
"The Pygmies" (Koasati), pp. 247-248. Smithsonian
Institution Bureau of American Ethnology Bulletin 88.
Washington, D.C.: United States Government Printing
Service, 1929.

John R. Swanton, Smithsonian Institution Bureau of
American Ethnology, collected these myths and legends
between 1908 and 1914. He interviewed Alabama and
Coushatta in Polk County, Texas, and Coushatta near
Kinder, Louisiana. His primary sources were Celissy
Henry, George Henry, and Charles Martin Thompson.

Bibliography

Abernethy, Francis E. *Tales from the Big Thicket*. Austin: University of Texas Press, 1966.

Alabama-Coushatta Indian Reservation Web Site Online, 1999.

Albers, Patricia and Medicine, Beatrice. *The Hidden Half*. New York: University Press of America, 1983.

Apache Web Site Online. Purplehawk's Nest, 1999.

Atkinson, M. Jourdan. *Indians of the Southwest*. San Antonio: The Naylor Company, 1935.

Banta, S. E. *Buckelew the Indian Captive: The Life Story of F. M. Buckelew While a Captive Among the Lipan Indians in the Western Wilds of Frontier Texas*. Mason, Texas: The Mason Herald, 1911. New York: Garland Publishing, 1977.

Babb, T. A. *In the Bosom of the Comanches*. Dallas: Press of John F. Worley Printing, 1912. New York: Garland Publishing, 1977.

Berlandier, Jean Louis. *The Indians of Texas in 1830*. Edited and Introduced by John C. Ewers. Washington, D.C.: Smithsonian Institution Press, 1969.

Bierhorst, John. *The Mythology of North America*. New York: William Morrow and Company, 1985.

Boatright, Mody C. *Mexican Border Ballads*. Dallas: Southern Methodist University Press, 1946.

Caddo Nation Official Web Site Online, 1999.

Carlisle, Jeffrey D. "Apache Indians." *The Handbook of Texas Online*. Austin: The Texas State Historical Association, 1999.

Canonge, Elliot. *Comanche Texts*. Norman: University of Oklahoma Press, 1958.

Carter, Cecile Elkins. *Caddo Indians*. Norman: University of Oklahoma Press, 1995.

Champagne, Duane. *Native America: Portrait of the Peoples*. Washington, D.C.: Visible Ink, 1994.

Cremony, John C. *Life Among the Apaches: 1850-1863*. Glorieta, New Mexico: The Rio Grande Press, 1868, 1969.

Deloria, Vine Jr. *Red Earth White Lies*. New York: Scribner, 1995.

Dennis, T. S. *Life of F. M. Buckelew*. Bandera, Texas: Hunter's Print House, 1925. New York: Garland Publishing, 1977.

Dobie, J. Frank. *Legends of Texas: Texas Folklore Society* Vol. 3. Hatboro, Pennsylvania: Folklore Associates, 1924, 1964.

Dorsey, George A. *Traditions of the Caddo*. No. 41. "Introduction to the Paperback Edition" by Chafe, Wallace L., 1997. Washington, D.C.: Carnegie Institution of Washington, 1905. Lincoln: University of Nebraska Press, 1997.

_____*The Mythology of the Wichita*. "Foreword" by Elizabeth A. H. John, 1995. Washington, D.C.: Carnegie Institution, 1904. Norman: University of Oklahoma Press, 1995.

Fehrenbach, T. R. *Lone Star: A History of Texas and the Texans.* New York: Macmillan Publishing Company, 1968.

Foster, Morris W. *Being Comanche: A Social History of an American Indian Community.* Tucson: The University of Arizona Press, 1991.

Gelo, Daniel Joseph. *Comanche Belief and Ritual.* Doctor of Philosophy Thesis. Ann Arbor: University Microfilms International, 1986.

Green, Rayna. *Women in American Indian Society.* New York: Chelsea House Publishers, 1992.

Hirschfelder, Arlene and Molin, Paulette. *The Encyclopedia of Native American Religions.* New York: Facts on File, 1992.

Hook, Jonathan B. *The Alabama-Coushatta Indians.* College Station: Texas A&M University Press, 1997.

Jones, David E. *Sanapia: Comanche Medicine Woman.* New York: Holt, Rinehart and Winston, 1972.

Lankford, George E. *Native American Legends: Southeastern Legends: Tales from the Natchez, Caddo, Biloxi, Chickasaw, and Other Nations.* Little Rock: August House, 1987.

La Vere, David. *Life Among the Texas Indians: The WPA Narratives.* College Station: Texas A&M University Press, 1998.

Lipscomb, Carol A. "Comanche Indians." *The Handbook of Texas Online.* Austin: Texas State Historical Association, 1999.

"Lipan Apaches in Texas." Texasindians Web Site Online, 1999.

"Lipan Apache." Whitestareagle Web Site Online, 1999.

Malone, Prairie View. *Sam Houston's Indians: The Alabama-Coushatti.* San Antonio: The Naylor Company, 1960.

Marriott, Alice. *The Ten Grandmothers*. Norman: University of Oklahoma Press, 1945.

Martin, Howard N. *Myths and Folktales of the Alabama-Coushatta Indians of Texas*. Austin: The Encino Press, 1977.

_____"Alabama-Coushatta Indians." *The Handbook of Texas Online*. Austin: Texas State Historical Association, 1999.

Moore, R. Edward. "A Little Basic Anthropology." Texasindians Web Site Online, 1999.

Morfi, Fray Juan Agustín. *History of Texas: 1673-1779*, Part I and Part II. Albuquerque: The Quivera Society, 1935.

Numuukahni/Comanche Lodge Web Site Online, 1999.

Newcomb, W. W. Jr. *The Indians of Texas*. Austin: University of Texas Press, 1961.

Noyes, Stanley. *Los Comanches: The Horse People, 1751-1845*. Albuquerque: University of New Mexico Press, 1993.

Paterek, Josephine. *Encyclopedia of American Indian Costume*. New York: W.W. Norton & Company, 1994.

Perttula, Timothy K. "Caddo Indians." *Handbook of Texas Online*. Austin: Texas State Historical Association, 1999.

Reading, Robert S. *Arrows Over Texas*. San Antonio: The Naylor Company, 1960.

Rollings, Willard H. *The Comanche*. New York: Chelsea House Publishers, 1989.

Rothe, Aline. *Kalita's People: A History of the Alabama-Coushatta Indians of Texas*. Waco, Texas: Texian Press, 1963.

Shaw, Charles and Bradshaw, Reagan. *Indian Life in Texas*. Austin: State House Press, 1987.

Smith, F. Todd. *The Caddo Indians: Tribes at the Convergence of Empires, 1542-1854*. College Station: Texas A&M University Press, 1995.

Stone, Merlin. *Ancient Mirrors of Womanhood*, Vol. I and II. New York City: New Sibylline Books, 1979.

Sultzman, Lee. "Comanche History Part One, Part Two, Part Three." Web Site Online, 1999.

Swanton, John R. *Myths and Tales of the Southeastern Indians*. Smithsonian Institution Bureau of American Ethnology Bulletin 88. Washington, D.C.: United States Government Printing Office, 1929.

_____*The Indians of the Southwest*. Smithsonian Institution Bureau of American Ethnology Bulletin 137. Washington, D.C.: United States Government Printing Office, 1946.

_____*Source Material on the History and Ethnology of the Caddo Indians*. "Foreword" by Helen Hornbeck Tanner, Norman: University of Oklahoma, 1942, 1996.

Waldman, Carl. *Atlas of the North American Indian*. New York: Facts on File, 1985.

Wallace, Ernest and Hoebel, E. Adamson. *The Comanches: Lords of the South Plains*. Norman: University of Oklahoma Press, 1952.

Wichita & Affiliated Tribes Web Site Online, 1999.

Wright, Muriel H. *A Guide to the Indian Tribes of Oklahoma*. Norman: University of Oklahoma Press, 1951.